# Narcissist Free

*A Survival Guide for the No-Contact Break-Up*

## Zari Ballard

Also by Zari Ballard:

**_When Love Is a Lie_**
*Narcissistic Partners & the*
*Pathological Relationship Agenda*

**_Stop Spinning, Start Breathing_**
*Managing the Memories That*
*Keep Us Addicted*

**_When Evil Is a Pretty Face_**
*Female Narcissists & the*
*Pathological Relationship Agenda*

ISBN-13: 978-1502462237
ISBN-10: 1502462230

# Dedication

*To my readers & blog visitors:*

*Everyday, you inspire me. Everyday, you show me that we are all sisters and brothers and we're in it together. For you, I am forever grateful.*

# Table of CONTENTS

## *Note to Readers:*

In this book, when I refer to narcissists, sociopaths and psychopaths as being of the male gender, it is only for the sake of convenience and because I speak in great detail about my own relationship experience.

Certainly, narcissists and psychopaths do not exist only as boyfriends and husbands. They can, in fact, be male or female and come disguised as wives, girlfriends, mothers, fathers, sisters, brothers, sons, daughters, bosses, and co-workers. Whether the N/P is male or female, all issues from the victim's perspective are equally important and just as distressing as any relationship described on these pages.

That being said, this little book of No Contact is dedicated to any **woman or man** who is being (or has been) subjected to emotional manipulation by a narcissist or sociopath and seeks a way out. Although it's a club to which none of us want to belong, as long as we're here, let's do what we all do best: *try to figure it all out.*

Only this time, we'll do it together…

With hope & sincerity,
Zari

# Narcissists &
# The Game of Life

In the Game of Life, players that have a narcissistic personality will always play by a different set of rules than everyone else on the game board.

To normal players, the point of the game – which is reflected in the rules – is not as much about winning as it is about collecting as many happiness points as possible without bumping other players. If, by the roll of the dice, a player happens to bump another player, it is usually with regret and the player may choose, at that moment, to forfeit the move or continue ahead. Whether the normal player chooses to play as a single player or in relationship mode with another player, the point of the game, for the most part, never changes.

The narcissistic player, on the other hand, always plays in relationship mode yet secretly moves through the game determined to win completely on his own. To hide his intention, the narcissist may begin the game disguised as a normal player, whereby reducing – and even eliminating – the chance of his partner catching on, dropping out, or having him booted from the game. He may even switch partners mid-game without either player knowing – a game strategy that is intended to cause emotional confusion and increase his overall chances of winning.

To the narcissist, who views the finish line very differently than other players, the point of the Game of Life is all about how many players he or she can bump off the game board while still moving forward…. and *fuck* the happiness points.

# *Introduction*

Breaking up with a narcissist is never easy but, with the right intention and the willingness to let a few things go, it certainly can be done. The good news is that the "rules" of breaking up with a narcissist are completely different than the rules that apply to even the most dysfunctional of "normal" relationship break-ups. When you break up with a narcissist, there are a whole slew of things that you simply *do not* have to worry about.

For example, when you decide to finally quit a narcissistic partner for good....

- You don't have to worry about hurting his feelings because he doesn't have any
- Because he's never around, you really don't even have to *tell* him you're breaking up
- Even if you do break up in person, he'll likely be so insulted (narcissistic injury) that he'll start giving you the silent treatment anyway
- You don't have to worry about running into him anytime soon because of his Houdini-like ability to vanish off the face of the earth
- And so forth and so on.....

Of course, in order to *really* break up and truly let go of the narcissist, you, as the victim, have to be able to give up a few of the things that have been keeping you from breaking up with him in the first place including:

- …the need to have the last word because it will ever happen. The narcissist is a *walking dictionary* of last words and he'll always have a better one.
- …the need to hear him confess and admit to every awful thing he's ever done to you because he won't have the slightest idea what you're talking about
- …the need to first get reimbursed for all the money you've either spent on him or he's "borrowed" from you because, again, he won't have the slightest idea what you're talking about
- …the need to have him grovel for forgiveness because, in the blink of an eye, he'll have *you* groveling for forgiveness and you won't even know how he did it
- …the need to break-up but then *still* get closure-style revenge (somehow) because chances are he's already thought ahead and his revenge on *your* revenge will be much worse
- …and so forth and so on

Yes, ending a relationship with a narcissist is easier than you think because the reality of the situation is that you've been broken up the whole time! Just because the narcissist disappears without saying a word doesn't mean he hasn't broken up with you – because he *has*. Silent treatments are just break-ups in disguise *intended* to make you *imagine* that the possibility that you haven't been dumped for good still exists.

Recently, I received a heartfelt email from a reader who wondered if No Contact still counted if she decided to implement it during a silent treatment. Of course it does! You can turn a narcissistic silent treatment around anytime in your own mind just by saying "This is *not* a silent treatment. This is No Contact and I've just dumped *you!*" My point is that, since the narcissist is never around anyway, you can break up with him anytime simply by *not being there when he gets back.* You can just as easily block *his* phone and change *your* phone number - as he does to you - but you must do it with one thing being very, very different: **the intention.**

Again, the silent treatment is a narcissist's way to avoid you dumping *him* by keeping you confused as to whether or not he just dumped *you.* He *intends* to return because his *intention* - always – is to keep you from moving on from the pain he has caused (although he's been moving on the whole time). You have to understand how the narcissist is really thinking - the evilness and indifference of his plan - and accept it as truth. Because it is, in fact, the truth! Once you grasp the facts…that he doesn't and *has never* loved you, that he's perfectly happy playing this cat and mouse game forever and ever, that he will never change and, therefore, wanting revenge and closure or to hear one more disingenuous "I'm sorry" is just a waste of precious time…once you really, really *get* all of this, it will become amazingly clear to you that dumping the narcissistic partner is far easier than you ever thought possible.

Now, when you co-parent with a narcissist, things are slightly different but only *technically* and I discuss this in detail in *Chapter XIII: The Co-Parenting Dilemma.* The truth is that narcissists are no better parents than they are partners. Narcissists walk out on their families to be with other partners all the time and don't have the slightest problem doing it. No problem at all. So, if you don't have the strength to end it while he's still living with you, then wait for him to leave (and you know he *will),* change the locks, tell the kids, and start the process of divorcing his ass.

I'm not saying that your decision to finally break-up for good isn't going to be sad – because it will be. What I am saying is that, if you stay focused and mean what you say and say what you mean, to *actually break-up* with the narcissist, to end it, to stop the insanity once and for all *isn't going to be that hard.* The hard part is always *within us* – the victim – and it *always* has to do with our inability to be honest with ourselves about the *intention* of the "break-up". If your plan, deep down, is to go No Contact in hopes that he will end his silent treatment, you may as well just sit and wait for the hoover **and** save yourself the trouble. He's going to do all those awful things narcissists and sociopaths do whether you love him or not, remain loyal to him or not, wait for him or not, or break-up with him or not. So you may as well break-up with the motherfucker and quit his unlovable ass. And going No Contact (NC) – as hard as it appears to be in theory – is the only strategy that ever works.

For all those who have read my first book, **When Love Is a Lie**, and perhaps my second, **Stop Spinning, Start Breathing**, you should already understand that I'll mince no words in my mission to get my point across. I've taken a lot of flack for using four-letter words and so forth but my books are what they are because they are based on real life. I don't see any purpose in holding back when it comes to this topic so for all those with sensitive ears, heed my warning. It may get fucking crazy so either exit the ride or buckle up. Those who know me from my books or from visiting my website know without a doubt that I truly care and that is what counts above all else. I will also be including – as I did in **When Love Is a Lie** – stories from other women and men who have written to my website to share their experiences. These posts will be noted, italicized, and shaded in grey. I think it's extremely important that we all learn from each other and, specifically, that you, as a reader, have more experiences than just mine to draw from.

The strategy of going No Contact is nothing new for anyone who has searched the internet for answers to the nightmare that is narcissism. The truth, however, is that going No Contact - by its true definition - does mean that this particular break-up is the last one. Committing to NC means that you've had enough and that you want your life back. It means that you're willing to suffer through what you already anticipate will be sad, sad days spent lamenting what could never have been. It means ignoring hoover upon hoover upon hoover (i.e. attempts by a narcissist to solicit a reaction) because you absolutely realize that *giving in* means certain emotional suicide. Going No Contact means that you mean business. Once and for all.

So, with all that being true, it felt natural and necessary to spend at least a chapter or two reminding readers of *why* NC is the key to the rest of your life....*why* the narcissist that you love and *must leave* forever is and always will be completely different from any "normal" human being you have and will ever meet.

So, let us begin....

# Part I:

## Why You're Here &
## Why No Contact

# *Chapter I:*
## *Aliens Among Us*

At any given moment, there are literally millions of emotional vampires walking this planet disguised as human beings. We may know them as narcissists, sociopaths, or psychopaths but, believe me, they are separated by only six degrees of evilness. Each is but a horse of just a slightly different color and, if we happen to love them, there is no difference at all.

Those of us who share the experience can well understand that there is something significant that makes us very different from them. We understand that this difference is far bigger than the fact that this person is a complete jerk and we're not. We understand that having a narcissistic personality means that something at the core of this person's very being is missing and that it's this "lack of" that gives the narcissist the capability to do what he./she does to the people who care about them. We also understand that there is no way for this person to simply obtain this missing ingredient or to "get it back" and this is what causes the grief that we feel. We realize that a narcissist can't "get back" what a narcissist never had and, consequently, at the moment that we make this discovery, the relationship becomes a done deal and all efforts made after the fact to "fix" this person will be futile indeed.

So, what is it that someone who has a narcissistic

personality lacks? What is this core human element or ingredient that, without it, transforms these walking, breathing monsters of emptiness into something even worse? And how did it happen? Is it possible that it never developed or perhaps it was never there to begin with or, even worse, is it possible that a person with precursors to narcissism can, at some significant moment in time, choose *not* to nurture this quality from within, whereby willfully allowing it to die an instantaneous death? What the hell *is it* anyway??

The missing ingredient, my friends, is *empathy*. Yup, good ole' empathy....the core element /quality/ingredient of human-to-human goodness that can be defined in a zillion different ways that all mean the exact same thing. For example, here are just a handful of definitions for **empathy** that I found online while doing some research for this book:

1.  Identification with and understanding of another's situation, feelings, and motives.

2.  the imaginative projection of a subjective state into an object so that the object appears to be infused with it

3.  the ability to mutually experience the thoughts, emotions, and direct experience of others.

4.  the capacity to recognize emotions that are being experienced by another sentient or fictional being

5.  the power of understanding and imaginatively entering into

another person's feelings

6. The ability to understand another person's circumstances, point of view, thoughts, and feelings

7. the ability to understand the thoughts feelings or emotions of someone else.

8. the awareness of the thoughts, feelings, or states of mind of others, perhaps by means of some degree of vicarious experience of others' feelings or mental states.

9. the experience of understanding another person's condition from their perspective.

10. The ability of a person to place themselves in "another person's shoes", so to speak

Yes, empathy is what a "normal" person has (or feels) that narcissists, sociopaths, and psychopaths do not. In fact, it is this lack of empathy that is key to every single thing that is wrong with the N. When a narcissist is part of a couple and the other person is "normal", it is this lack of empathy on the N's part that will ultimately cause all of the suffering. You may have even heard of the "normal" person – or victim – in the relationship referred to as an *empath* on certain websites/forums that are actually run by sociopaths and narcissists. On these websites, the behaviors of *empaths* are openly mocked and deemed as weak and annoying. Yes, I believe the narcissist knows *exactly* what he's missing and he's quite proud of it.

Now, as I stated in **When Love Is a Lie**, just because a narcissist isn't capable of *feeling* emotion doesn't mean that he can't comprehend its importance. To compensate for what he can't (and doesn't care to) feel, a narcissists very cleverly learns to *pretend* and *impersonate,* mimicking the emotions needed to blend seamlessly into society. But, as you and I both know, some emotions are easier to fake than others and pretending to really care about someone is simply not that easy. Even for a narcissist. The fact that they can do it so well shows us how ingrained in the ideology they really are.

Now, to be clear, empathy is very different from *sympathy* and, in order to understand how seriously lacking in humanism a narcissist really is, it's important to make the distinction. A narcissist can fake sympathy but he can never, ever fake empathy and when he does try, he fails miserably.

When a person feels empathy for someone else or for someone else's situation, the feeling comes from *our experience.* When we appreciate what another person is feeling because we've *been there*, been in his shoes, or felt that exact same feeling at some point – and maybe even at many points – in our lives, we can do much more than sympathize with this person. For example, when my son was born, he was very ill and remained in the hospital NICU from birth until he was almost seven months old. It was an extremely traumatic period that was always intensified by the fact that he could, at any time, get unexpectedly sicker and die.

During that time, I became close to the parents of other NICU babies and we empathized with each other in a capacity that is beyond words for me even now. To describe what myself and the other NICU parents felt toward each other's situation as sympathy doesn't even come close.

The same applies to any of us who experience a situation – good or bad - that touches us on a personal level. When we happen across another person in that same or a similar situation, we draw from our own experience automatically and *feel* for that person. This is why all of us who have been involved with a narcissistic partner can relate to each other on the level that we do. This is also why those who have never had the experience simply don't "get it" and probably never will. We can't really blame them for this because the complexity and passive-aggressive nature of this type of emotional abuse has to be experienced for a person to even fathom that it exists at all.

I think, eventually, as we get older, we automatically start to empathize more than we sympathize simply because our archive of meaningful experiences grows bigger. A narcissist, on the other hand, is completely incapable of feeling empathy because *he has no archive to draw from.* Although he may have had similar experiences as someone else, he lived through his experiences *feeling nothing* and, therefore, this is exactly what he brings to his understanding of the experiences of others – **nothing**. He simply can't relate. He might *try* to relate – for a minute – but it never lasts. My ex would disappear at the beginning of any crisis – *no matter how small* – that pertained to me or my life and he'd resurface only when he felt enough time had passed that the situation had resolved itself or someone else had helped me out. Seriously, if I mentioned to him on the phone that my car had broken down, he'd literally become a no-show for at least a couple of weeks or until I drove down to find him *in my car*, thus signaling that the crisis had obviously ended and his assistance was no longer needed. This is the type of bullshit that becomes completely predictable!

If you think about it....how on earth does a narcissist live his/her life? Imagine if *you* were a person who could basically *feel nothing* and a zillion circumstances kept occurring where you were expected to feel *something* and where everyone around you was obviously feeling something *other than what you were feeling* which was complete annoyance at the inconvenience of having to feel anything at all!! I can't even count the letters and emails I've received from women whose narcissistic husbands, for whatever reason, never even made it to the births of their own children or who found a reason (i.e. new narcissistic reply) to leave the home and abandon the family just shortly thereafter.

The fact that a narcissist *can't feel*, to me, is reason enough to leave these monsters. Sure, if we really wanted to, maybe we could muster up some *sympathy* for this inability to be human, but why do that? Why should we even *try* to figure it out...to help this person…to save the relationship…when the simple truth is that a narcissist *can't* feel and this *isn't* a fixable problem? The narcissist doesn't care that he can't feel because he knows that he can fake *almost* whatever emotion he needs it to get what he wants. It's usually when the attempts of a narcissistic partner to fake empathy begin to fail miserably that we notice the slip of the mask and start to seriously wonder *what the hell is going on.* It is the narcissist's amazing ability to fuck with us emotionally that makes the entire relationship *appear* to be so utterly complicated. I use the word "appear" because I made a discovery just recently that narrows the pathological relationship agenda down to two simple intentions combined in a singular process. The truth is that narcissists are as simple as they are complicated.

Allow me to explain….

## Chapter II:
## Simplified Evil

No matter from what angle we examine a narcissist or sociopath, the view appears complicated. Of course, he'll swear up and down that "complicated" is *far* too exaggerated a description and the problem, of course, is us, *right*? Consequently, when a narcissist scolds us for making mountains out of molehills, it's his attempt, as always, to make us doubt our intuition (gas-lighting) and, for the most part, this tactic serves the narcissistic ideology accordingly. Or does it?

In **When Love Is a Lie**, I describe one altercation with my ex where he made the statement, "Really, you're making me out to be complicated and the truth is *I'm just a simple man.*" Finding his self-description very clever, he then used *I'm just a simple man* as his new catch phrase for every argument where he felt he had to defend himself. It wasn't until much later, after receiving mail from readers describing similar circumstances, that I realized, by insisting "I'm really just a simple man", my ex was – albeit inadvertently - providing me with the biggest clue *ever* into how these jerks really think. Because the behaviors of the narcissist are so mind-boggling and so out of the norm of how we might consider behaving toward someone we care about, we tend to trump them up, making the behaviors much more complicated than they really are, thus actually giving the narcissist too much credit in the long run! I now believe – as of today – that there are really only **two reasons** that a narcissist acts the way he does towards his partner and everyone around him *and they both have to do with control*. In fact, everything that confuses us about why the N did what he did, why what he did continues to hurt us, and why it appears that he's not doing it to everyone else (which, of course, he is or will be eventually) can be broken down into this *control factor*.

Everything – and I mean *everything* – a victim partner is subjected to during a relationship with a narcissist (N) happens for either/or of the following two reasons: 1) as a means **of controlling** that person, or 2) as a means **for validating** that control. That's it! That's all it is! You have to keep in mind that it's *the relationship* that's complicated – and only for the victim. The narcissist himself/herself, in reality, isn't all that complicated. We just view him or her as complicated because, as normal, loving human beings, we wouldn't even consider doing what they do or saying what they say.

A narcissist's main concern in life is to control the people around him – namely, us - so that he gets what he wants, whatever that may be. In order to control, of course, he has to manipulate our reality and mirroring our good qualities back to us is an excellent way of hooking us into the Lie. As explained in the last chapter, we must never forget that these people are *imposters of the emotional kind* and they're very good at what they do. To get what they want (i.e. adoration, ego boost, sex, money, etc.), a narcissist will tell us *exactly* what they know we want/need to hear to make it happen. Even when he or she is being as sweet as pie (which is, of course, a façade), the narcissist is *controlling* us. Then, once the narcissist gets what he wants, he starts a fight, creates chaos, cuts us loose, disappears, subjects us to the silent treatment or the cold shoulder, erases us as if we never meant a thing, and generally makes us feel like shit - tactics that are fully intended to manage down our expectations of the relationship for future go-rounds.

It is the victim partner's **reaction** to this "managing down" process that ultimately *validates*, for the narcissist, that his control is still solid even when he doesn't need that person. When a narcissist succeeds in riling us up to the point that he can actually *feel* our desperation and codependency, then his control is validated and he can go about his business secure in the fact that we'll be around when and if he *does* need us. And around and around it goes.

This particular control/validate process can happen in an hour, several times a day, over two weeks, or over many years. It's a push/pull system that translates to control/validate, control/validate, control/validate until we're ready to lose our minds. For the narcissist, it's a way to secure future narcissistic supply and that's really all he cares about.

Maybe what appears to *us* to be well-thought out,

calculated manipulations to wreck us really boils down to the narcissist either *controlling* us or *validating* that control – or, for that matter, controlling others (i.e. the other women) or validating *that* control. Maybe a narcissist really *is* just a dumbed-down sociopath (like sociopaths proclaim)and we've been giving him far too much credit in the intelligence department! I'm fairly convinced that this is the key to the narcissist's psyche.

Mind you, my little discovery in no way pardons the narcissist for his despicable behaviors or for causing everyone – and even his own children – so much pain. He is absolutely guilty as charged. And if, in fact, I'm right and narcissists – like my ex - really do believe in the simplicity of their own evil, then that makes these losers even more unfixable than ever before. And, believe it or not, the fact that a narcissist's evil agenda is not nearly as complicated as we've perceived it to be is very good news. It would mean that we no longer have to think so hard about *why* he does what he does. It means that we now need less of a reason to stay because we have one more very important reason to leave….to go No Contact…to get out of this very emotionally dangerous situation.

This book is about knowing – finally – that it's time to get out. It's about realizing it's time to save the rest of your life because *this **bad** is as good as it's ever going to get.*

**From: Darcie**

*I have been in a friendship with a person who I suspect is an N or maybe has those tendencies-I'm not really sure. We have been friends for about 2 years and while we haven't had any real arguments or disagreements, I have been on the receiving end of the silent treatment from her periodically. I will usually attempt to contact her a few times then I will just let it go. I am 45 years old & have been through this game before with former friends and boyfriends when I was younger. I don't really have time nor am I going to react in the childish manner she probably expects from me.*

*I didn't really know what was going on the first few times it happened. She would usually contact me after a while with some really lame excuse. I would usually just blow it off. I had no idea what I could have done wrong. I have finally started to see a pattern. It will usually occur over something as simple as me being the one to end a phone conversation 1st or forgetting to call her at a certain time, or not being able to answer my phone when she calls. For example, she got really irritated one day when I did not answer right away when she called. I had my phone in another room on the charger. She left me a pretty scathing voice mail which seemed out of character for her. I just let it go & she hasn't done that again.*

*She is married & has a whole other group of friends that she has never introduced me to so I admit that there is probably a side to her I don't even know. She seems to like to keep her life compartmentalized & segregated for some odd reason. The only clues that I have that she may have some N characteristics are the silent treatment thing, her extreme tendency to dominate conversations for hours on end, and her tendency to want to position herself as a type of guru to others. Also, when you start to think for yourself & not give the utmost respect for her advice or you disagree with something she has said, then you will get the silent treatment. When she does resume contact again, she can be very intrusive and call at all of hours of the day and night. We have never really had an argument but these things are really weird. Another really strange thing is she refuses to meet any of my own family. She will drop me off at my home but refuses any social invites that involve any of my family members. I don't get that.*

*Does any of this sound like potential Narcissistic behavior? I wonder if I was more involved in her life whether or not I would see more N-type behavior? I will admit that I had a very negative feeling the 1st time I met her but later dismissed it as me being judgmental. I remember thinking to myself that 1st time, "Who does this know-it-all think she is?"*

*I'm seriously thinking about ending the friendship because this silent treatment & passive aggressive behavior is getting on my nerves. Do you have any advice?*

**From: Me**

*I am so sorry for what you are feeling...the confusion and bewilderment at what I absolutely believe to be behaviors indicative of a narcissistic personality.*

*The silent treatment....and the reasons you describe: it will usually occur over something as simple as me being the one to end a phone conversation 1st or forgetting to call her at a certain time, or not being able to answer my phone when she calls. For example, she got really irritated one day when I did not answer right away when she called. are* **exactly** *as I have experienced and as countless others have experienced. I was* horrified *to miss a call because I absolutely knew what the repercussion would be. We all experience this – exactly. Ludicrous and hurtful behavior, obviously, but so, so typical.*

*Also, her unwillingness to meet your family (and socialize that way) and the compartmentalization of what is most likely a second, secretive (for whatever reason) life or lifestyle....all of this is crazy-making narcissistic behavior that will never change no matter what you do or say. Moreover, if you don't end it, she never will and the games will play on, continually getting worse...because this is what a narcissist does. Nothing you or anyone else will ever be able do can change her. She likes herself just the way she is and feels nothing but justification in treating you badly. A narcissist is incapable of friendships or meaningful relationships of any kind and will choose a person as a target (as I believe you were chosen) specifically because this person has all of the qualities that they are incapable of having. Then, they will do everything they can to cause chaos, drama, hurt feelings, uncertainty, insecurity, you-name-it with all types of passive-aggressive measures...in effect, they will begin to destroy you.*

*It's not worth it. End the friendship and be done with it. Either call her or write her or however you want to do it but tell her, in very clear terms, that you refuse to be subjected to silent treatments and other nonsensical behaviors any more and that the friendship is over. Don't allow her to engage you in an argument because she will only twist the truth and manipulate and she is a Master at both. If she starts to argue or blame, just be calm and say "This isn't open for discussion and I'm not going to argue with you. The fact is that you feel that it's okay to behave like that towards a friend and I don't – it's as simple as that – so there's no reason to drag it out. Take care and I have to hang up now." The conversation should be no longer than maybe five minutes or a letter no longer than one side of a piece of paper. You don't owe her anything much less to waste your breath trying to explain something at length that she is incapable of comprehending. Make it short and sweet and then go No Contact.*

*Especially when it comes to any involvement with a narcissist, the rule is to go with gut feelings every single time. You are spot-on with your analysis of this person and your instinct is telling you to end it. Go with it. And, believe me, it is the right decision. Don't waste another second of your time because life is too short for any of this crap.*

## Chapter III:
## *Knowing it's Time*

*When Love is a Lie* and particularly in *Stop Spinning, Start Breathing*, I spend quite a few chapters discussing the narcissist's worst characteristics…the traits that make him the narcissist that he is. I also explain the importance of creating relationship deal-breakers so that the next narcissist that approaches you on a romantic level gets the royal boot or – better yet – falls away of his weight simply because he can *feel* the presence of boundaries. Whether we like it or not, the fact that we had no boundaries whatsoever made us an easy target for narcissistic love-bombing. A narcissist, as we now know, can smell a boundary-free victim from miles away and he will pounce if he finds this person even the least bit attractive. Even more appealing to the narcissist is a victim who appears confident, fun, and crazy sexy but who, underneath it all, is boundary free. This, my friends, was *you*.

I don't care what anyone tells you – when you met the narcissist, you weren't lacking in self-esteem. In fact, it was your self-esteem that drew him to you….your spontaneity, clever sense of humor, and amazing intelligence. You may have shared a common interest…something other women he'd recently met had no particular interest in (at least not at the level he'd hoped for) and this caused a spark in the narcissist's stale brain. It created a connection that he could feed upon which is what a narcissist does best. He feeds upon the things that you enjoy by making them things that you could enjoy together (at least during the love-bombing stage). Later, of course, he'll find a perverse way to twist this "love" connection into something evil that you'll actually feel threatened by without really knowing why. This is all part of the plan, of course.

And how did he get away with all this manipulation in that short span of love-bombing time? Well, he rested on the fact that you – in all your confidence – had inadvertently forgot to create relationship deal-breakers and boundaries. And he was in like flint.

I would be willing to bet that most of you who are reading this right now have know for a long, long time that this "relationship" with this person that you love has simply got to end. And by "end", I mean *really* end...as in *over, finished, done, and any other word that describes a finality.* However, the narcissist has a way of knowing this as well and so he has likely kicked his deception into high gear as a way to intercept and distract from what we know we should be doing. The narcissist, after all, doesn't really want the relationship to end – at least not until *he's* ready and can call the shot himself – and, therefore, he will lie until he's blue in the face so that *nothing* gets in the way of his fun.

But for you, knowing that it has to end means coming face to face with the many, many reasons why and this is never easy because there are *so many*. Nonetheless, you must accept them as the unfixable facts that they are and use them as a guideline for getting into No Contact mode. And here we go....

You know it's time to end the relationship with the narcissist and go No Contact when:

- *....the end of your relationship is never-ending. In other words, it ends a lot but, in reality, it never ends. He is always leaving you – whether he's giving you the silent treatment (a break-up in disguise), accusing you of everything he's doing, blaming you for every problem the two of you have ever had, disappearing for no reason whatsoever and reappearing for the same, or whether he's just plain treating you like a piece of shit. It's time to call it quits.*

- *...you can't let go – no matter how bad he treats you. You may want to let go and you may even put your foot down and end it yourself every once in awhile but the truth is that the fury and scorn is but fleeting and you are horribly addicted to the very drama that you hate. The narcissist knows this, of course, because he created it and so he accepts the vacation with a smirk and waits for you to grovel back (which you always do). It's time to stop this ridiculous insanity.*

- *...you've become a booty call, a buddy fuck, a friend with benefits, or however you'd like to describe it but the truth is he leaves you, lies to you, hurts you, abuses you, neglects you, abandons you, cheats on you, all this and more AND he still gets to sleep with you. Not acceptable under any circumstances.*

- *...except for maybe in the beginning, you've never felt like a couple. Either you do nothing together at all (like my 13-year relationship) or he's made a point to have an entirely separate life that you know nothing about and will never be a part of (like my 13-year relationship) or something similar. The fact is that when you don't feel like part of a couple with the person that you love, you just fucking know it.*

- *...you've become a super-sleuth, a master investigator, a private-eye extraordinaire when it comes to uncovering the lies and deception of this person who supposedly loves you, yet you really know nothing about him or what the fuck he's really doing when not with you at all! What you've become is an expert at wasting your own time and, as a result, your life is slowly slipping away. No one should ever make you feel suspicious 100% of the time – ever! It's time to stop the cycle of your own abuse to yourself.*

- *...you cry more than you smile. No need to elaborate further.*
- *...you can't remember the last time that you smiled.*
- *...the needs of your children are starting to interfere with your obsession time and, even though you know this, you can't stop the feeling that you just want them to go away so that you can wait for his call in peace.*
- *...you've inadvertently – and maybe even deliberately – become not only a stalker and a snoop, you've become one of those girls that gets down on her hands and knees screaming for forgiveness from a partner that treats her like shit for something that was never, ever your fault. If you do this even once (and we all have at least a **thousand** times!), the show, unfortunately, must come to an end.*
- *.....you find yourself willing to forgive him for anything just to have the separation anxiety go away. Your gut tells you he cheats on you (even if you haven't been able to prove it) and you take him back. He disappears and then reappears with a completely illogical story and even though you don't exactly jump up and down when he shows back up, you don't tell him to fuck off and go away either. He'll go for long stretches without answering your calls or texts (for no apparent*

*reason) but if you, by chance, happen to miss
answering one of his calls, all hell breaks loose.
The rules are completely different for him than they
are for you...and you allow it.*

Any one or all of the above relate to your situation? If so,
it's time to pull the plug on this relationship once and for all. The
fact that we put up with even one of the above scenarios is utterly
ridiculous. Do you understand this? Read over the red flags above
and really look at each one. When the "love" that we feel becomes
all about the suffering, it simply ceases to matter at all. Do you
understand this? How can we claim to *know love* at all when the
love that we're deliberately immersed in is so fucking sad? Did it
ever occur to you that this love that you use for an excuse to stay
with the N isn't really love at all? Think about how possible that is
considering what we all imagine love to be!

The narcissist that we think we love has never loved us.
This being true, we now know that love was a lie. It's time to get
out so that we have a chance to experience real love before we die.
We owe ourselves this and so much more.

Do you understand this? I think that you do. Now, if we
could only figure out a way to break the *mental connection* we
have to this false love. To do this, we need only to understand
it...so let's take a good look....

# Chapter IV:
## The Mental Connection

I'll be the first one to tell you that there are certain people in our past – former boyfriends, girlfriends, husbands, and wives – that do not deserve to be hated forever and maybe not even at all (depending upon the situation). I'll also be the first to say that somewhere down the road, after the pain has passed and time has healed our wounds, it would even be entirely possible to rekindle a friendship or at least to co-exist on the planet on a level beyond being merely civil. The narcissist is not a person in our past that we can even think to include in a rekindling scenario. It just isn't possible.

The narcissist, of course, in his attempt to "guilt" you out of No Contact will, of course, play the "let's be friends" card, making it out to be entirely possible that the two of you can break up and remain buddies. Trust me, this is not a possibility if for no other reason than the fact that he was never a friend of yours to begin with. Remaining friends with the N will do nothing more than keep you attached to the problem even if you feel strong going in. The fact is that you are going to be the only one extending any wisps of friendship. Eventually, you will find yourself feeling that awful pang of anxiety as soon as your eyes open in the morning. By lunchtime, you'll be staring at the phone, letting other calls go to voicemail lest you miss his call or text and make him angry because you didn't answer right away. By dinnertime, you'll be freaking out because he didn't call and you may even begin to call him…over and over and over and over. When he does finally pick up, he'll ask "What the fuck is your problem anyway?" and then, when you start to whimper or get huffy about the fact that everything seemed fine the day before and why didn't he call to at least say hi, he'll be silent for five terrifying seconds and then he'll say calmly with just a touch of smugness in his voice, "Why? I don't have to call you at all. Don't you remember? We're just friends now."

And don't even consider being just fuck buddies with the N either because then you've really committed to go down the rabbit hole. While it may seem at the time that at least he's only sleeping with you during the break-up, the truth is that he's not – he's still sleeping with everyone only now he gets to sleep with you too. If your boyfriend or girlfriend is a narcissist, trust me, he or she is cheating on you and probably has been for most of the relationship. Do not be delusional about this fact just because the sex was exceptional (if it was). I had exceptional sex each and every time for 13 years with my ex and I always thought this is what held us together. Little did I know that he was having that same exceptional sex with countless others. To a narcissist, great sex is great sex. There is no mental connection on his part and that's why he can do what he does with no remorse and no regret. This is why he feels justified in being the asshole that he is.

As a break-up strategy, No Contact is as powerful at it is because of the mental connection that we have to the narcissistic partner. If we don't break the mental connection, we can never even hope to get better let alone live a life with any kind of normalcy. And it's not extreme to compare your attachment to the N to that of a drug addict to a drug because both and you and I know (all to well) that it certainly feels like the worst kind of addiction. When he's with you immediately upon his reappearance from a vanishing or silent treatment, there's a kind of quasi-high that feels like an instant awakening. The fog miraculously lifts. All of the anxiety goes away and you can actually laugh and smile and all that good stuff. No matter what he did or was doing while away, as soon as he's back, the weight that lifts makes it all worthwhile.

Up until that point, you're likely inconsolable, heart-sick, and consumed with everything that has anything to do with him and, for many of us, this is a completely crippling time that nothing outside of a dose of the N can fix. I was always my skinniest self during a silent treatment because I couldn't eat a bite and even if I did, my anxiety would burn it off. It felt, literally, like my nerve endings were on fire all of the time. Again, nothing about this break-up is normal because nothing about the entire relationship and about the type of abuse is sane in any sense of the word.

In order to have any chance at all of getting this guy or girl out of your system, you simply must put distance between yourself and the situation. What many victims do not "get" about No Contact is the fact that as soon as you declare that you've gone NC, you are in complete control! And when I say "declare", I actually mean that you've made a commitment to yourself mentally and that you are going to follow-through on each and every rule for as long as it takes to get better. I'm not saying that you can't or won't cry or indulge in personal pity parties…I'm just saying that you are taking any and all communications and contact with the narcissist out of the equation. In doing this, you will finally be creating an environment that nurtures recovery. The narcissist doesn't even have to know what you've decided because he'll know soon enough.

The breaking of the mental connection is first and foremost in the break-up strategy itself and this is why the act of blocking his number, whereby making it impossible for the N to call or text, is so powerful. Trust me, I hear from many men and women who have gone NC and this "blocking" element causes the most angst. They'll tell me they've gone NC but continue to ruminate on whether he's texting or not texting or if he's tried to call or if he's not calling and I'll listen to this for a minute and then I have to ask, "Well, have you blocked him? Because if you block him, you won't have to worry about any of that." For so many, it's like a light bulb flicks on and the next time I hear from these people, they're amazed at how peaceful the silence is and their only regret is that they hadn't done it sooner.

What we don't realize while we're in the relationship (and right after we get out of it) is the sheer magnitude of the time we actually spend waiting for the N. We're either waiting for a text or a call or for him to come over or whatever. To keep us in a constant state of heightened anxiety is the intention of each and every strategy in the narcissist's pathological relationship agenda. These strategies, obviously, are as deliberate as they are effective. When we actually make a move to block this person from being able to implement his evil, life simple begins to change. Suddenly we can do whatever we want because we take all the reasons for thinking about or waiting for his text or call completely out of the equation. Think about it....how many times have you not done something you needed or wanted to do because you were stressed about missing his call or text and what the inevitable punishment of that might be? Forget the fact that he never had to answer his phone or respond to a text from you if he didn't feel like it. What a fucking double standard that was! Believe me, the "block" will set you free!

**From: Marielle**

*I know how it all works - manipulation, gas-lighting, baiting, triangulation, lies, deceit, abuse, begging for him to stay, and then finally being discarded. Looking back on the whole 15-year mess, I know that No Contact is the only way to go. Yet, instead of feeling better as time goes on, I've gone from being strong to wanting him back...to wanting him to chose me again.*

*Non- stop thinking of him and what we used to have together (and I do know we never really had anything). My head knows all these things but my heart is a mess all over again. He got to me, he really did. He had written and told me he wasn't with the new woman (only, I'm sure, for me to cancel the child support issue). When I ignored that, he left a horrible message on the machine saying that they were back together and I was messing things up. I know exactly what he was doing and I know exactly why I should have just deleted and not listened to any of it because now I'm obsessed all over again that he is with her and not me.*

*Right now, he's on holiday and meeting her in Hawaii (my most favorite place). I swear to you – it's just about made me suicidal all over again. Even though I know that was an elaborate plan on his part, it worked perfectly. I'm right back where I started in February. I keep thinking things like "Why did he do this to his family?" when, of course, I know why and "Why couldn't he have chosen me?" when I should be happy that I'm free of his web of manipulation and abuse. The pull is so strong and no one understands. I have lots of supportive friends but no one can help me. No one has a clue as to how much these people take hold of your life and feelings. I've had many friends say that I can stop these feelings but I can't. I've been brainwashed and I'm co dependant on his abuse. But no one understands- not even me.*

*I'm back in the fog and I haven't seen or spoken to him since February. Yes, there was that time I texted twice after much baiting which I know is the reason that I'm back here again. I took the bait. I know all these things! But Zari, I'm finding life incredibly hard at the moment. I have a very nice man trying very hard to date me and he is a gentleman and treats me so well but I'm not one bit interested in him. All that I know is a world of abuse and begging and drama. It's such a bizarre feeling to think that I'd be happy to go back to that (when really I'm not ). It's the most hopeless feeling around and, honestly, if I thought I'd feel like this everyday for the rest of my life, well, it's not worth going on for me. Yes, I know he's not worth it and I know I'm worth more that that. I know what he is but I just can't seem to let go!!!*

**From: Me**

*I am so sorry that you are so horribly sad and I do remember that feeling well. Yes, you are right - this whole thing was an elaborate scheme to wreck you before he left on his holiday and it's truly disgusting behavior. Narcissists know exactly what they're doing when it comes to stream-lining a victim's co-dependency and it is pure evil intention. THIS is what you must keep in your mind. Whatever you are feeling right now is NOTHING to what you would be feeling if he came back and then left you again to go back to her which is exactly what he'd do and you know it.*

*I am glad you have a nice man wanting to date you but I wouldn't suggest that either. I was SO where you're at right now and I tried the dating thing too soon and it backfired. Being with someone else made me miss the N so much that I dumped the nice guy without a word and acted just like the N!!! On that, I would hold off because you and I both know that it would just hurt your heart more.*

*Your ex is a narcissist through and through and, of course, he is with her and better her than you! I know it's hard to feel that you've fallen back but you must pick yourself up and remember the relationship for what it is. The way he treats you is NOT NORMAL and he will not be able to treat anyone else any better in the long run. Do not think about that. Postpone the sadness until tomorrow and then tomorrow, postpone it again and keep going until you find yourself back in a good place.*

*As for the friends who don't "get it", they never will. The "hold" is incredible but stop trying to explain it to them because it will only make you feel sad and isolated. I got to the point after it was over where I stopped talking about it altogether with certain people and this actually forced me to "pretend" that things were okay with me. It helped to retrain my brain back to the "old" me and that wasn't half bad. Something has to give so that you are not ruminating and obsessing about this jerk. You must tell yourself that NOTHING HAS CHANGED since that time just recently when you were starting to feel good and in control – NOTHING. It only appears to be that way because that's how he has manipulated it and managed down your expectations. But you can go back to that point because you never left it.*

*Please postpone the sadness and do something nice for yourself. You deserve so much better than this jerk could ever give you!!!*

**From: Sammie**

*After many years with a man that didn't actually commit to me until more than a year or so of back-and-forth 'dating' that was ALL on his terms, he finally discarded me after he did his best to get me to just leave. He really didn't want to have to man up and dump me, so he did so over the phone. And one month after our break up (we were living together and had been together more than 6 years) I was informed he had a new girlfriend. So I allowed that to send me into an utter tailspin. After a serious car accident and legal problems, I was weakened when he actually contacted me and of course(!) believed he missed me. Well the final insult came after months worth of our instances of getting together while broken up (and, as far as I knew, may or may not have still been seeing his G.F.)..........I found out he was LIVING WITH this girl and....eventually that she was PREGNANT while he was texting me that he missed me and maybe one day we would work out. I am not over this pain, I'm still mortified it got this far. I'm devastated because this means it's really over (I know, I know). I'm seeing red when I'm not sad. I want justice and I want to punish him but I'm realizing there may be nothing to be done. I want to be over this, past this, beyond this. I feel like I have wasted A LOT of precious time, pining away for a person whom I am now learning may have*

*NEVER even loved me at all. And my newest issue is that I am dating someone new and now sort of paranoid that he may be fooling me too. I don't think this is the case, and I am pretty intuitive (trust me, my gut told me my recent ex was messed up but I chose what I thought was "true, real love"). I don't want to panic and ruin what I think is such a good thing. I also don't want to fall down another rabbit hole, master-manipulated by a narcissist.*

**From: Me**

*Your story rings so familiar not only with my own but with all of us who share their comments here. In my book,* When Love Is a Lie, *I am adamant that, whether we want to believe it or not, chances are high that the narcissist we love is not only* seeing *someone else while he/she is with us, he is most likely* living with *someone else as well.*

*One of the mistakes I made early on (and long before me and my ex ever ended it for good) was to try and get over him by quickly dating someone else. It didn't work. In fact, it made me miss the narcissist even more and, thus, I became even more weak and vulnerable and receptive to his eventual return. And, don't get me wrong, in looking back, I think that these were probably nice guys but I didn't even give them the chance before I acted just like the narcissist and blew them off. I wasn't ready to date and, honestly, you may not be either. It takes a while to grasp the reality of what just happened – the level of betrayal is not something you can get over simply by jumping into another relationship. Now, I have no way of knowing if this new guy is a narc is a narc or not but chances are high that you're going to believe he is anyway simply because you're not even over the old one. This has nothing to do with panicking...it has to do with being logical and giving yourself a chance to recover. If you're still thinking about revenge on the ex, you are in no way ready to see someone else. I've been there, done that and, believe me, it only seems like the best route to recovery but it really isn't.*

*Create boundaries and commit to keeping them and you'll be just fine in the dating world. Boundaries are our only protection against narcissists and other emotional predators and they will run in the other direction if they even get an inkling that you have them!*

# Chapter V:
# *Narcissistic Word Garbage*

I was thinking my ex today and about all of the incredible lies he told me. I remember how, as the years passed, I could see him gradually attempting to hone this particular talent right before my eyes. For example, to practice lying (I assume), he would tell at least one lie every day while, at the same time, deliberately leaving evidence of the truth – such as a store receipt – in plain view where I could find it. Whatever I would find would almost always contradict what he had told me. And, because I simply couldn't help myself, I'd have to address it and conversations would go something like this:

**Me:** Where did you say you bought that book?

**W**: What book?

**Me:** The book you bought yesterday…the one about making guitars.

**W:** I don't know…why?

**Me:** I'm just asking a simple question, that's all. I thought you said you bought it at Bookmans.

**W:** Then that's where I bought it. What are you getting at?

**Me:** The receipt says Barnes & Nobles.

**W:** So? What's the big deal? What are you accusing me of now?

**Me:** Well, it isn't a big deal and I'm not accusing you of anything. I'm just curious why you would make a point of saying "Bookman's" when obviously you were at Barnes & Nobles.

**W:** Jesus Christ! What's the fucking difference? Why does it matter?

**Me:** It doesn't matter! I just don't get why you would deliberately lie about something so stupid?

**W:** Oh please...I'm so sick of this...What are you doing? Snooping around my receipts now?

**Me:** I wasn't snooping, Wayne, it was right here on the counter.

**W:** Then obviously I wasn't trying to hide anything! Could we get past this please?

Word garbage! Look *to his lie* for the truth and therein lies all justification for walking away. I determined long ago, based on my own 12-year experience with a narcissistic partner, that pathological lying is a deliberate narcissistic/sociopathic strategy specifically used to get away with all the crap that a narcissist needs to get away with day to day. To tell a white lie here and there and only when absolutely necessary would do a narcissist no good because he is always up to no good and, therefore, it's necessary to lie all the time. In a narcissist's mind, the decision to lie as much as possible – if not all the time - is a no-brainer because it eliminates the possibility of him having to think too hard about lying *specifically*. By being a pathological liar, all bases are clearly covered. And although he may be *slightly* concerned about getting caught, he's only concerned about the inconvenience it may cause for those first five or ten minutes just prior to him initiating a silent treatment and disappearing into thin air. The fact that his lies have the potential to – and often do – cause great pain and suffering for the people around him (and particularly, his partner) doesn't even enter into the equation.

So, the joke often told on narcissist recovery sites *"How do you know a narcissist is lying? Because his mouth his open!"* is about as true of a statement as anyone can make about a narcissistic partner. Everything he does, everything he says, all those ludicrous behaviors that we ignore...all of that is based on the premise that he is, by choice, a pathological liar. Consequently, we can, if *we* so choose, spin ourselves silly trying to unscramble the narcissist's mixed messages but it won't give us anything better than what we've already got. In other words, it will never get better than the bad that we already have!

When our partner is a narcissist, we are constantly trying to figure out *why* and there's no need. We spend hour upon inconsolable hour praying to the Love God for answers but the truth is that we already know the answer....we just don't happen to *like* it very much...and that's okay. We don't have to like it. But, in order to be free, we *do* have to accept it as well as all the pain that comes with it. The good news is that, while the answer may be permanent, the pain that we feel *is* not. It will *go* away but *not* by avoiding it and only *after* we allow ourselves to feel it.

Stop sifting through the narcissist's word garbage for specs of truth when his pathological lie is the only truth you need...the only reason you'll ever need to go No Contact and distance yourself from this God-awful nonsense.

### From: Darianne

*I've recently been busy reading & researching NPD. It's so creepy - your book/website could have been written by me about my Narcissist! After splitting 6 months ago with this guy, I've experienced above all else the narcissist's rage and it's absolutely horrendous, Nothing but verbally abusive phone calls that have left me shaken, anxious & unable to sleep/concentrate. I decided to enforce the NC rule about 2.5 months ago following a particularly horrible conversation. I had assumed he'd get the message loud & clear (I mean, he's an intelligent guy right?) WRONG!*

*On my birthday, I received a delivery from Fed Ex and it was from him. Always expect the unexpected, everyone, because it wasn't a card, gift or an attempt to win me back. Oh no! It was a black & white canvas print of me in my underwear that I'd asked back for months ago. He was trying to not only prompt a reaction but to show me how I'd been disgraced. I don't for one minute think that receiving this on my birthday was a coincidence. He times it perfectly!*

*Following this delivery, I received a call from an Anonymous ID (I've blocked his number) with someone listening in silence and then hanging up after 10 seconds. Then, my Apple account was hacked & the password re-set...both events happening within 10 minutes of one another.*

*And this week, while I've been on holiday trying to escape the nightmare, guess what?! More contact! I'm not sure how he found out I was away but so far I've received 2 calls, a voicemail, a message on WhatsApp (now blocked), and 2 emails. The initial contact concerned a wedding we've both been invited to. I'd previously told him I'd be going so now he's was checking on that (yeah, right). The email was blunt but not rude, the WhatsApp message apologized for interrupting my holiday, and then voicemail said he needed to speak to me urgently.*

*I've managed to stay strong & not respond but its soooo fucking hard! Today I received an email bright and early at 6am which read "Your friends with Kate?? WTF is going on with you?" To explain, Kate is an ex-girlfriend of his who he'd painted out to be a complete psycho. In reality, she's a lovely girl who had a psychological breakdown after he discarded her. Makes sense to me!!! We've become friends & managed to support one another. Thankfully, she has now moved on & has a great BF.*

*My point here is that a narcissist will try ANYTHING to prompt a reaction. You can block numbers, change numbers, move 100 miles away probably and they'll ALWAYS find a way to get to you. No Contact is hard but absolutely necessary and I'm hoping a year on from now it continues to become easier to cope with. I love the fact it's our ONLY way of getting back at them & it sure does work!*

**From: Me**

*Thank you so much for writing because I get your message loud and clear……You have the solution, girl, and you just keep doing what you're doing because, as hard as it is, you are doing everything right!*

*It's all about getting a REACTION and he sure has tried, hasn't he? One reaction is all it takes to put a narcissist back in the driver's seat in his twisted mind. Why give him that? You are so right to turn to your support group of friends as a way to get around it. And for those who don't have that, come to websites like this one and others where there's a world of virtual friends waiting to help. Wonderful advice….*

**###**

**From: Karen**

*I felt the need to write tonight…I'm going to see a therapist on this Friday because I feel like a mixed up bag of crap. As I was writing things down to discuss with her, I flipped to some things I was writing in my journal about things I've noticed that wasn't right about him. I had 12 things at the time, but believe me by the time the relationship was over there were plenty more. I started crying asking myself "why, why didn't I leave him then?" He was ALWAYS disappearing or not answering the phone, but would turn around and tell me that I was controlling and a drama queen. I would ask him to explain how I was both, but he never could give me any reason.*

*I thought about a particular event one evening when I spent the night over to his home. This night we did not have sex or anything and because of his snoring, he slept on the couch and I slept in the bed. When I starting making up the bed, I found a hair pen in the bed...I walked in the living room and slammed it on the table and replied I found a hair pen in the bed. This jerk got fuming mad and was like, "don't start that shit Lisa, that's probably (the grand daughter's name) or YOUR hair pen." I was like I don't wear hair styles that require hair pens and the grand daughter hadn't been over. He went on to say that he doesn't even sleep in the bed and he doesn't know how it got there, etc. I was sooooo hurt, but guess what? I actually started thinking "Did I have a hair pen in my head???" Crazy huh? This is why I'm going to see a therapist cause I'm wondering how in the hell was I so gullible. I'm like SOOOO angry with myself. Obviously this bitch didn't even have the decency to change the damn sheets because she could have saved me the pain of finding that hair pen. Right now I want revenge on him so bad but the Lord said vengeance is his. I've gotta get through this...*

**From: Me**

Come on....are you sure you weren't seeing my boyfriend??? LOLOL Sounds so frigging familiar. I, too, found something in my ex's bed – a broken piece of a bracelet and I did the same thing, demanding answers, and he kicked my ass and threw a livid fit. I call these particular "fits" **distraction reactions** because they are specifically intended to turn things quickly – and they do. Before I knew it, I was apologizing because – hell – maybe it was my bracelet (it was not, of course!). Either way, I chose to go the easy route rather than face the truth. Just one more thing that I stuck on the backburner....for what? So he could do it again? We all do it and you're not – nor have you ever been – crazy. These guys are very good at what they do or they wouldn't be narcissists.

You're in good company, girl. There are literally thousands of us scratching our chin, wondering what the hell happened? It's hard to accept the truth but just know it was never ever you. He's just a monster, plain and simple.

### ###

**From: Brandy**

I had a situation this past week end. My N took two of our daughters to my older daughter's house for the week end. So, he knew I was alone all week end. He stalked my house, blew up my cell phone and then got real nasty with me because I didn't respond to him. I refuse to respond to his nastiness anymore.

*Anyway, here's how it went Tuesday: I made the mistake of asking him what time he was picking the girls up for dinner! I am No Contact with him unless it's for our kids:*

**Him***: so, are we hung over*

**Me***: what are you talking about*

**Him***: you had a busy week end, how was your trip*

**Me***, what the fuck are you talking about. I was home because I have the flu!*

**Him***: You weren't in the house when I was in it!*

**Me***. You weren't in the house*

**Him***: how do you know*

**Me***: cause I was fucking here!*

**Him***: Where were you Friday @ 11 and Saturday @ 10 pm*

**Me***: Home*

**Me***: Where were you at those times, Mike?*

**Him***:  in our house looking for you and you weren't there!*

**Me***: Liar, liar, liar!*

*Him: How do you know?*

**Me***: Cause I was home, you idiot!*

**Me***, there's only one part of truth here and that is, you were around this house (stalking) but not in it!*

**Him***: Again, how do you know?*

*Me: I was here. When you're ready to speak the truth, then talk to me.*

**Him: Look who's talking about the truth! That's funny!**

*He's a sick man... I even told him how sick I was feeling and that I didn't want to fight and it simply didn't matter.*

**From: Me**

*So glad to hear from you and good for you for sticking to the NC! That being said, this guy is so typically narcissistic, it's ridiculous. What he's doing is reacting to the NC. There's nothing a narcissist hates more than indifference! The lying is just him being his pathological self – what an asshole. The good news is that he has obviously come to the conclusion that you mean business and this is the reason for the TYPE of reaction he's having. If he hadn't have come to this conclusion, he'd be hovering in a much different way. HE KNOWS YOU'RE ON TO HIM which is a very good thing. But that also doesn't mean you have to put up with this crap. Now that you know he's just reacting in narcissistic fashion, go right back to not engaging with him in any way except for when it relates to the girls. In other words, you just continue on as you've been doing because YOU'RE WINNING! Honestly, I doubt very much he was even on your property at all. He was throwing that bullshit out there because he knew that the girls were gone and you, therefore, could have done whatever you want (and, boy, does he hate THAT although HE does it all the time!). My ex did that ALL the time ("I got a phone call from your boyfriend this weekend" when I had no boyfriend or "I drove by and your car was gone...did you have fun fucking around?" when I was home the whole time). Typical. Typical.*

*I'm so sorry that you don't feel well and he doesn't need to be making that any worse. If he calls, the second he says anything non-children related, hang up. Thank you for the update and keep them coming.....*

Word garbage is word garbage, sisters and brothers. We've been fooled and manipulated. We've been flat-out conned into believing the bullshit and doubting cold-hard evidence. No contact eliminates this from happening. The silence from taking out the word garbage is going to retrain your brain recognize this bullshit so that it never happens to you again.

Not convinced yet? Okay, let's talk some more about why you feel connected to the very drama that you hate.

# Chapter VI:
# *Trauma Bonding*

Feeling attached to a narcissist or sociopath even though he treats us badly is a constant source of angst for those in recovery from toxic relationships. Victims want to know why…*why can't I just let go? Why can't I move on? Why do I feel so connected to someone who feels no connection to me?* One logical answer to this is that we're normal and *they're not* and normal people want to fix things that are broken so that they work again. The problem of course is a narcissist can't be fixed because he never was right to begin with. In essence, the narcissist isn't broken at all. He simply is what he is and what he is no good. This being true, what do we do, after a Discard, when we can't shake the feeling of being only ½ a person without him…of feeling utterly attached even when we're apart and even when he's with someone else? Why can't we disconnect from the Bad Man? Well, there *is* an answer to this for those who seek a deeper psychological reason for the suffering and it's a condition often referred to as trauma bonding.

When we think of trauma bonding, we typically associate it with The Stockholm Syndrome (TSS) – a condition named after a situation that occurred in XXXX where a group of hostages became attached to their kidnapers. TSS, however, although certainly similar to trauma bonding, typically occurs in life-threatening situations where the victim is literally in fear of dying at the hands of her toxic, abusive partner. Trauma bonding is more descriptive of the attachment dilemma that occurs from the type of trauma caused to our *emotions (i.e. **betrayal and neglect**, over and over and over)*. It's the type of bonding that can easily occur via passive-aggressive manipulation (i.e. sex, lies, silent treatments) and other forms of narcissistic control.

The narcissist partner, as cunning as he or she is, *understands the process* for streamlining a victim's codependency to point of least resistance. He has actually figured out – without a single day of formal training - that the best way to ensure narcissistic supply is to create trauma bonds with his targets via the method of "seduce and discard".

The conditioning that leads to trauma bonding focuses on two powerful sources of reinforcement reoccurring in succession over and over and at perfectly timed intervals. Psychologists call this reinforcement the *'arousal-jag'* which actually refers to the *excitement before the trauma* (arousal) *occurs* and *the peace of surrender afterwards* (jag). Take a second to reflect on the narcissist's behaviors. Creating trauma bonds is what he's been doing his whole life!

'Arousal-jag' reinforcement is all about *giving a little* and then *taking it away* over and over and over in *well timed intervals*. Narcissists do this all the time (disappearing/reappearing, silence/chaos) whereby creating an illusion of twisted excitement that reinforces the traumatic bond between us and them. And to be clear, the narcissist feels a connection here as well only *his* connection is to the excitement alone and not to us. This is why a narcissist always has multiple partners because it doubles and triples his excitement factor. The fact that we – along with others – become so attached to the chaos that we wait for his return is quite an added bonus!

Are you getting it yet?? Stay with me here because I'm gearing up for the punch line to our co-dependency!

The excitement before the trauma (of betrayal and neglect) is created during the **devalue stage**…that point in time right before **a discard** when our intuition has already told us he's going to leave based on his behaviors. It's that knot-in-the-stomach feeling, the overwhelming urge to cal his phone 100 times…. it's that urge that I would get to write letter upon letter begging him not to do it… it's the hours spent scouring the internet looking for clues or doing drive-bys in the middle of the night….it's the feeling we get from the chaos that a narcissist ALWAYS creates right before the storm. Whether we want to admit it or not, we become highly addicted to this narcissistic nonsense and we miss it like a motherfucker when it's gone….when, suddenly, it all goes silent. We *long* for the connection – as manipulated and fabricated as it is – until we can barely breathe. Then, right before we commit hari-kari, in swoops the narcissist once again – seemingly back from the dead like a Phoenix rising – to give us **the second reinforcement:**

***the peace of surrender that happens afterwards***. His reappearance is meticulously timed for maximum effect and usually follows a silent treatment that has lasted just a tad longer than the one before. The narcissist is conditioning us to accept less and less so he can get away with more each time he vanishes.

Either way, this second dose of reinforcement – the peace of surrender – is absolutely heaven! Again, it's an addiction - to the make-up sex, the vanishing of our anxiety, and the feeling of calmness and euphoria we get from *knowing* that, *once again*, we've been given a reprieve to breathe until the cycle repeats again. Seduce and discard…seduce and discard….till the end of all fucking time. And, at that moment, we're actually okay with that! In fact, there's nothing in the world we'd rather be doing.

During the silence of my own break-up with a narcissist, I have come to realize that my ex worked very, very hard at trauma bonding (as I'm sure your ex or soon-to-be ex did as well). In my case, silent treatments would run two weeks on/ two weeks like clockwork for months at a time and with no explanation. Then, to compound the insanity, from mid-October to mid-January – every year for 13 years - he made like Houdini and fell completely off the grid. Right before he'd leave, he'd always ramp up the chaos, making me feel horribly anxious and angry at his peculiar and suspicious behaviors yet, at the same time,  desperate for his attention. I was fucking addicted to all of it and he knew it – and none of it was ever that good! This guy knew *exactly* what he was doing!

Our addiction to the chaos and *then to the reprieve* also explains why we find it so hard to move on into other relationships after the narcissist. No one excites us in quite the same way or with the same intensity as the toxic partner. Via trauma bonding, we become the suffering and the suffering becomes us. We forget what normalcy feels like. The chaos and turmoil becomes almost as big a turn-on for us as it does for the N.

But here's the kicker, girls, and some of you may already know this little tidbit. It's actually a scientific fact that *women are biologically susceptible* to trauma bonding…and it all has to do with a bonding hormone (actual term!) called Oxytocin. Yes, that's right, there appears to be a biological reason why it's so easy for us to become addicted to the narcissistic nonsense. While this doesn't excuse our susceptibility, I found it nonetheless interesting. Oxytocin is the actual chemical that starts the birth process…the chemical that, by preventing *memory consolidation*, allows us to forget the pain of childbirth to the point that we'll actually choose to have *more* children. I found this fact to be frigging amazing. Memory consolidation, actually, is very close to the phenomena that I refer to as *relationship amnesia* -our ability to forget what it is about the narcissist that makes him such a bad person. *Relationship amnesia* (discussed at length in my book ***Stop Spinning, Start Breathing***) is part of the mental connection that keeps us addicted and oxytocin, it appears, is part of the reason it happens. However, since an adorable baby is the reward for the pain of childbirth and there *is no* reward for the pain caused by a narcissist, I am only providing this information as an interesting side note and not as an excuse for why we're here. Trauma bonding is created by a very clever captor to keep his victim co-dependent and, believe me, narcissists know exactly what they're doing every second that they're doing it. It is part of the evil of narcissism and an enormous part of why we must go No Contact and end the madness.

### From: Janice

*My counselor told me this week that I was dating a narcissist for 4 months. He ended it 4 weeks ago which doesn't sound like the norm. Wish I'd had the empowerment to do it, he chipped away at my self esteem. He was charming and everything I thought I wanted...at first. Handsome, foreign with an accent, sexy, athletic, charming, generous. He bought me flowers, no guy ever had before, was generous with his things, we had great sex, but at times I wondered if he was sexually addicted. But I always thought and felt something was off and couldn't figure out what it was. He'd criticize what I wore, bras, panties, t-shirts, jeans, shoes, my couch, home, everything. So I tried to please him and no doubt those leaking moments showed him that I was under his thumb. He'd criticize others when we were out—especially fat people. I never introduced him to my parents knowing he'd find fault with them and I couldn't bear to have him criticize them as they're elderly with dementia.*

*When he drank he would get drunk, always ignoring his own words, "I'm not going to drink tonight." He didn't like me to drink socially. Every TV show, movie, or restaurant would be his choice, nothing ever about me. When we'd go shopping it was all about what he wanted for himself, quite the dresser and wore tons of cologne. I remember we were shopping for boots for me it took us over an hour to find something both he and I liked. He did a lot of social media and texting. His preferred communication was texting and I felt closer to him when he'd text or call. But in person he seemed different. I'm curious if narcissists relate better via email, text, than in person? When we'd be in a group of people I questioned why he wasn't the same way with me. People loved him because he was charismatic, funny. Then we'd be by ourselves it was a different guy and I'd be hurt. It appeared he was texting and having conversations with other women and I could never figure out how he knew them. In hind sight I think some were former girlfriends. It appears that's his pattern. It concerns me now seeing people post that he'll contact me again. He's left quite a good computer trail using his real name on sites rather than an alias. I've seen that he already has a female "follower" on a music site. It has been so helpful to see other here post that something seemed wrong but couldn't figure out what it was. He was always cutting me down. When I'd stand up for myself we'd go round and round about the most ridiculous things. Sarcasm and cynicism were his preferred methods of "humor" and then he'd attack me for not getting his sense of "humor". Does narcissism occur because of abuse and alcoholism in his family or something that happened because of failed relationships?*

**From: Me**

*Everything that you describe about your Narcissist is part of the typical narcissistic pathological agenda. Yes, a narcissist relates better via text, email, etc because, unlike being face-to-face with someone, he/she finds it a helluva lot easier to be the Pretender that he/she is. This is why social media and online dating, among narcissists, is so popular. Communicating in this manner allows a N to live a double life if necessary (live with one person while texting someone else... and so forth). If possible, refrain from following him on social media because that is exactly what he wants you to be doing. It will make you crazy and keep you from moving on even in then slightest way.*

*One of the things I talk about in my book is the N's ability to act completely differently in the global arena (i.e. with everyone else) than he does with his partner. This is typical behavior. And it is the norm for the narcissist to leave first. In fact, the N loves to do the discarding and the more hurtful the discard, the better. If and when he does return (and, yes, they usually do at some future point), **it will only be to ensure that you never move on from the pain he has caused you.** Don't believe a word he says – he is a pathological liar.*

*As for why N's become N's, I can only give my standard answer: Who cares? In the end, why does it really matter why a monster is a monster? Knowing why is never going to change him. Being understanding of his past and problems is never going to change him. From here on, you must be the focus of your attention. You deserve so much better than he could ever give you.*

**From Janice:**

*Am out here reading today so I can remember how bad it was. Am having thoughts of him today. It has been 3 weeks since I checked and googled him. The longer I go without knowing the better. Am not sure why he's circulating in my thoughts today. The last I checked on him he was out on his latest woman's FB page commenting on her in-home wine business. How convenient for him so he can get drunk on her money and it will look legit. His double standard with me was he didn't want me to drink while he did. I had messaged one of his women from 2 years before me. I'm sure that's was weird for her and she didn't reply. At the time I was sorting out what was true and what was false. Now I realize most of it was false. Little by little situations creep in my head. Like the time he told me his company cut off his email and could no longer reply. Another way to discard slowly. I'm on an online dating site but realize not ready to date. I thought I was. I've had what is probably a nice guy contact me. I told him I'm not ready for a romantic relationship, maybe it's the fear coming out. Online meeting is disappointing so fulfilling the time left and will let it expire. Need to take care of me right now. A relationship will bring up co-dependency issues and until I have a better mindset on those I want to be solid in who I am. I need some fun in my life and am seeking out strong women friendships. Can't deal with anything that is draining right now.*

Now that your memory has been refreshed and adjusted, it's time to put the misery and discomfort behind us and move forward into a new and necessary phase of your life. You deserve it and, trust me, *it's going to happen.*

# Part II:

# No-Contact Strategies –
# Get it Started, Make it Stick

# Chapter VII:
## Understanding the Rewards

Going "No Contact" (NC) is all about you and this is something you must never forget. NC will give you all of the things that you've been wanting throughout the nightmare that was/is your relationship with the narcissist. It will give you back the much-needed control of your life that the N worked so hard to strip away. It will give you the elusive "closure" that you continually found yourself seeking during a silent treatment or whenever he walked out the door and literally fell off the grid, never to return. It will give you the peace and the silence that comes with a normal life. It gives you overall clarity about everything and allows you to see the relationship – and the narcissist himself – for exactly what he is. It instantly ends the vicious cycle of abuse that has become the norm in your life. It will allow you to establish boundaries that will ultimately prevent the nightmare from ever happening to you again. The list goes on and on. When the person we love (who doesn't love us back) is a narcissist, nothing less than good can come from going No Contact.

Going NC is more about restoring your sanity than it is about leaving the narcissist. Nothing about the ending of this relationship is normal and therefore nothing that you've ever been feeling – and nothing that you feel right now – is normal and NC can fix this. In order to move on...in order to actually be able to enjoy the life that you deserve, you must mentally fix the damage that the narcissist has created. The only way to do this is to completely cut off any and all avenues of communication with the N once and for all – and this is what going no contact is all about.

In *Chapter VIII: The No Contact Rule*, I'll give you the exact details of the no contact process. For right now, I want you to focus on what this rule really means and why it is the key to your future survival as a sane human being. Knowing what we know about the narcissist's behavior pattern and given the fact that the spectacle of your suffering, to the N, never ever gets old, implementing no contact and sticking to it is the only chance you will ever get to put distance between you and the relationship. Without distance, there is no hope of recovery. Without distance, there is no hope of you ever getting over the hurt. Without distance, there is no hope of you ever maybe meeting someone in the future who will love you in the way you deserve to be loved.

I remember being completely torn about going no contact. For one thing, as soon as my ex even suspected that I might be considering an escape, he'd immediately begin saying what I needed to hear. Like most narcissists, he appeared to have the uncanny ability to sense when I was getting my power back. I mean, he would take a silent treatment as far as it could go until he knew, without a doubt, that I had passed both the anger and sadness phases and had now moved into the power phase – a phase that, in essence, meant that I was moving out of my pain and into normalcy and he'd have none of that! Even as I started to feel better, I'd have that knot of anxiety that he was going to show up and ruin the whole damn thing. I knew that even though I was feeling better, it was still too early to say that I would never take him back. In fact, during this time, I would hope and pray that wherever he was, he'd stay there long enough for me to fully regain my confidence. But it rarely happened. I'd finally be feeling good for longer than a day and – BANG – here he'd come, tapping at the door with that familiar knock and resetting me back to the mouse that he left just a month before. A narcissist can *sense* when an ex is feeling stronger and, when he does, he'll quickly rearrange his newest situation (i.e. start a fight with the new girlfriend) so that he can maneuver a quick pitstop back into the ex's life to mess things up. Don't ask me how they do it…all I know is that they can - and will – do this almost every time. No Contact – if implemented correctly and with all boundaries in place – will fix much of the problem of this perfectly timed return.

The biggest reward of NC is silence. Victims don't understand this as a reward until they really tighten the reigns and remove the narcissist's avenues for gaining access into their lives. Once this is done, it becomes very clear why NC works. Suddenly you're not worrying about or waiting for a text to come in because *he can't text you.* Same with emails and phone calls. Preventing him from coming to your front door is a bit harder and involves either ignoring the knocks until he goes away or going to a local courthouse to get a temporary restraining order (usually for one year). The good news is that, while the latter option *is* a definitive (albeit extreme) way to make it stop, the truth is that most narcissists prefer to text, call, and email because these methods of getting your attention – or pushing your buttons – take the least amount of effort and, therefore, it's unlikely he'll take the extra step.

The rewards many and the emotional impact of each one runs very deep. When you implement No Contact by putting everything into place, making sure that the narcissist in your life can not – to the best of your ability - get to you, doors of freedom open up. Once you get past a few days (or weeks) of the initial sadness, victims usually have an "a-ha" moment that tells them "Hey, guess what? You can do whatever you want right now without worrying about being punished next time he shows up. Why? Because you've made it so he can't show up!"

Trust me, friends. Committing to No Contact is like giving yourself a big, comfy blanket of protection against the one person in your life who never cared about protecting you at all.

**From: Ann Marie**

*Well, when I wrote you the last time, I was starting NC and empowered. I felt strong and in control and avoided his calls and texts at all costs. But I wasn't quiet ready for the slur campaign against me and I'm going to honest and say it hurts. My crime, I guess, is that I'm still No Contact after 14 weeks. How dare I not answer his demands! In his letters to stop me about child support, I heard all about his new relationship and how it was finished. Then tonight, on the phone, he's saying things like "I'm starting a future with her!" I have his number blocked but messages still go to my message bank on my work phone. I'm actually surprised at the lengths he's going to try and get me to make contact although I have been reading about that. The pure venom has been incredibly hurtful and I guess nothing prepares you for it. But then again, I've never NOT done what he's asked of me and it's very empowering yet still very daunting. I have no trust in anyone anymore which is sad. The fact that he fits just about every criteria for textbook narcissism is what allowed me to read what he had in store for me next. Anyway, each day brings something new and I just try and go with it. Some days are better than others. I refuse to let him take another day of my life or of my children's lives. Do you believe he had the balls to say to me today karma will get me?! Let's just hope karma is real because as I know who will really get it . Thanks for listening!*

### From: Me

*How typical that one minute he's yelling that his new relationship is over and the next minute's he yelling about his future with her. This is why I always say that a narcissist lies even when the truth is a better story. Every day, all day, all the time....it's all one big Lie. Better her than you, girl.*

*And, sure, the smear campaign is incredible and what he's doing doesn't surprise me one bit. However, I don't understand why you even know what he's saying about you. I do believe that it's in your best interest to cut him off altogether so that he gets the message once and for all. As long as he has even one avenue of contacting you in any way (letters, texts, emails, phone calls, voice mails), you haven't gone No Contact. As long as he's able to even think he's contacting you (by thinking you'll be listening to messages, reading texts, opening letters), you haven't gone No Contact. No Contact means no contact. This means, for you, that you **block him completely** from calling, leaving messages, and/or texting you at home, on your cell, or at work. This means, for you, that his letters are returned to him UNOPENED with the words "Return to Sender" written across the front in black magic marker. This means, for you, that you stop all contact/freeze friendships with anyone who is privy to what he is doing without you or what he saying about you. No more mutual friends that he can send messages through. There has got to be a way to block him from one of the phones at your work – either your direct line or the phone at the main switchboard. With a little research on the system, I'm sure you'd find it's as simple as dialing \*## followed by his number. If that fails, get a Restraining Order/Order of Harassment that prevents him from contacting you at work. Where there's a will, there's a way.*

*You see, going No Contact means that he can't get to you AT ALL. It's really more about preserving/nurturing your well-*

*being than it is about anything else. One woman who writes here had been listening to messages and reading texts too, still thinking she was officially No Contact until I reminded her what NC really meant. Today, she wrote to say that she had finally cut him off at every angle and that it felt amazing because suddenly everything went quiet. Suddenly she wasn't sitting around "waiting" for his next hoover (because, whether we know it or not, that's what we're doing when we go partial-No Contact). To go "partial-no contact" indicates that you're just giving him the silent treatment and it has the wrong intention. Believe me, the narcissist KNOWS this. The narcissist KNOWS EXACTLY WHAT HE'S DOING. In your case, he knows all the nasty things to say that will get a reaction – any reaction at all, negative or positive. He doesn't even have to SEE or HEAR your reaction as long as he can IMAGINE that you're having one. This is why even the listening and reading has to end. There is no reason in hell why you should have to READ or LISTEN TO or HEAR ABOUT anything he says or does. As long as the legalities are in process about child support, it's out of your hands and let him argue with the court. He's obviously not a hands-on father so the excuse of co-parenting shouldn't be an issue. And you have to know that he's not going to all this trouble because he wants you back or has any feelings of remorse over anything. He left you for someone else and whether he's with her or not during any given moment, he has no right to even be contacting you. All he's doing is what ALL narcissists do – create constant chaos so that you never move on from the pain he has caused you. Maybe you need to make a phone call to his girlfriend and tell her to pull the reigns in on her man because he won't leave you alone! Better yet, the next letter he sends you (and the next and the next), stick it unopened in another envelope addressed to HER. Do that a few times and I bet the communications will come way down....*

*Hopefully, karma will get these guys but we certainly can't waste any more of our precious lives hoping to get a glimpse of it. Better to cut this jerk off completely and move on to the happiness you deserve, girl!!!*

**From: Ann Marie**

*Thank you... I do know that what you're saying is so true. I know that when I remained in No Contact, I was feeling stronger and better about myself. I was doing so well and I let the bastard get to me. I answered him via text on a emotional level - a level he'll never be capable of understanding. His messages to me were all about abuse and name calling as if he were standing over me. In one breath he'd say "Don't ever call me again" and in the next he's challenging me to call him. My family and friends want me to register his harassment with the police as they feel the worst is yet to come and that my children will be baited next. But I am now back in no contact I will not answer, look at, open anything, or discuss anything with him again. I need to get myself back together and move on and away from such a toxic human being.*

# Chapter: VIII:
## The No-Contact Rule

No Contact means exactly that – no contact. By definition, it can't be any simpler or complicated than it already is. No matter where you look on the internet, no matter how many books you read on the subject, no matter who you go to for advice on the narcissist recovery sites, you'll never get a different definition for what we refer to as The No Contact Rule. Consequently, what you *won't* find in this section is a long list of "do's and don'ts" that you've never heard before. All I can offer you is the guidelines that I know will make it work. There's no magic answer for going NC but you will discover that, indeed, it *is* the magic answer.

So, here you go:

**1. DO block, block, block.** This is the probably the most important strategy for beginning no contact because it eliminates the two most common of communications, the call and the text, with the text clearly being a favorite among narcissists. Narcissists love to text because it allows them to plan ahead for the desired outcome (whatever that may be)…to really think about what words would have the greatest impact on your psyche. As codependents to this crap, we get caught up in it ourselves. Everything becomes all about a text – either the writing and sending of it or the waiting and reading and then the responding to it. To the best of your ability, make it impossible for him to call or text you. And any landline, for those who still have one (I do), always has some capability for blocking numbers and one need only check with the service carrier to find out how. Usually it's as simple as pressing the # key, a two-digit code, and then the number of the person you want to block. I can't express how important the act of blocking is to NC. It seriously breaks the mental connection instantly (*See Chapter IV: The Mental Connection).*

**2. DO delete, delete, delete.** At the same time that you are blocking his/her number from any and all phones, you must also delete his name from your contact lists. This includes email, cell phone, address book and wherever you have the motherfucker's name written down.

**3. DON'T visit, spy, or stalk via Social Media or Dating Sites.** Going NC does NOT mean you can spy via Facebook, Instagram, Match.com and other sites. No creating fake pages under pseudonyms or sending messages through a friend's profile page. I've done *all* that and, believe me, it never works to make you feel better and his revenge on your revenge will be worse than you can ever imagine. By staying away from anything that has anything to do with him, we can finally begin to break the mental connection that keeps us addicted to the bullshit.

**4. DON'T attempt to contact or spy via proxy.** To contact or spy via proxy simply refers to the sending of any message or the harvesting of any information via human messenger. In other words, if you're feeling angry about the whole thing one night and decide to send a verbal "fuck you" message to the N via a mutual guy or girlfriend, this is breaking No Contact. *Tell James he's still a fucking asshole for me when you see him, okay?* The same goes for scribbling a letter and having someone else drop it in the mailbox, hand deliver it, or stick it on his car. The same goes for spending time with friends that you both know and deliberately dominating the conversation with your feelings about *him* so that the word gets back sometime in the near future. Just because you didn't come right out and *ask* for someone to relay a message, if you do this with the intention of it getting back (as it most likely would), your guilty of breaking this rule. Don't do it.

So many readers that have written to me will try to use "the mutual friend" excuse as somewhat of a reason why NC will never work. What they are actually doing when they bring this issue up is trying to justify leaving the door slightly ajar for running into or having to communicate or relay a message with the jerk in the near future. I refuse to see this as a viable reason for ruining the rest of your life.

This particular rule can actually get quite complicated which is why I chose to write a chapter about mutual friends for this book (*See Chapter XII: Cutting the Ties That Bind*) . The fact of the matter is that continuing to nurture or engage in relationships with friends that are also *his* friends does nothing more than keep the game going. That being said, sometimes it can be no other way so please see Chapter for guidelines in how to deal with it so that NC is not broken *because* of it.

**5. DON'T phone calls or emails. AND ABSOLUETLY NO TEXTING OF ANY KIND VIA ONLINE TEXT SERVICES SUCH AS PINGER.COM AND OTHERS.** Sure, we all no that there are free online texting services where you can send a text anonymously and even from a completely different phone number. I've been there, done that. he/she will know its from you and – POOF! – the control goes immediately back to the N. This defeats the entire purpose of No Contact and of you having finally taken back control over your own destiny.

**6. No sex, no kissing, no hugging, no shaking hands, no nothing!!!** Typically, by the time we're certain its over, it's because we know that the relationship is pretty much a farce. We know that the sex, even if its good, means absolutely nothing to the N because he can climb right out of bed and vanish with no problem. This being true, to think it's okay to touch this guy in any way after you've gone No Contact is ridiculous and defeats the entire purpose of the mission.

Now, if at any point during NC, you find yourself close enough to the N to shake his hand, you've obviously already crossed the line. However, its not a reason to give up. Many who make that first mistake view the next step into bed as a *Oh why the hell not…I've already fucked up just by seeing him* and I'm here to tell you that it doesn't have to be that way. You *can* come to your senses and climb back on the NC wagon instantly.

### *From: Janice*

*It has been 8 weeks since the breakup. Overall there have been good days. But the most troubling thoughts are still the sexual ones. The oxytocin levels were probably through the roof and now trying to cope without them. Unfortunately didn't help that I went back out on FB to mutual friends to see what he is "liking". I daily try to read something here or on the internet about narcissism, books on abuse, etc. to remember the way I was treated and how bad it was and could've been. Some days I feel like I was a fool. The good in the breakup is that I wake up in freedom now. That my weekends are my own and that I don't have to worry about what I'm wearing and whether something I wear will please him. Will it be the right color, cut. Is my hair long enough. Does he like my bra and my panties and then he didn't even notice when I bought new. I can watch what movies I want without having to watch a lot of military and violence. The prevalence of porn and how it's so easy to view it even on FB. Every once in a while a new thought of a situation will come to me and I'll think about what I'm learning about narcs. I think of the alcohol and the abuse of it and how I'm glad I'm no longer a part of it. Boring sitting in front of the TV not getting to watch TV shows I'd like to watch. But miss his arm around me. But try to replace that with remember how he cut me down. Told me I was being too sensitive about everything, he'd take his cell phone into the bathroom with him, how I'd never have cleavage or have lower body strength. Gees I'm a biker and a runner I have lower body strength.*

*One of the images I can't get out of my thoughts is when we went to a wedding reception for his co-worker. He went up to the daughter of the bride, in her mid- 20s, dressed in a very short, backless dress, and he placed his hand on her back. Such a suggestive move. He's friends with the wives of his coworkers on FB and it continues to frustrate me how he posts on the wives pages to get admiration supply. I wish the husbands would wise up. Something I'm wondering about: Do they remain at the same level and plateau or do things get worse. For example, view more porn, can't get enough sexual supply, drink more?*

**From: Me**

*So good to hear from you! I'm going to send you a copy of Book 2 (Stop Spinning, Start Breathing) which was written for those at the exact point where you are right now post-break-up. It addresses (and has exercises for) the managing of the memories, putting the relationship in its proper perspective, dealing with relationship amnesia, setting boundaries once and for all, all that working through the pain stuff. You can work through it at your own pace and I really think it will help you now that you've come this far. You'll like it and it will help you deal with things one at a time. Now, though, I'd love to comment on a few of your statements because I related to your words immediately:*

**".....told me I was being too sensitive about everything, he'd take his cell phone into the bathroom with him".** *Mine did the same damn thing. Makes me sick!*

**"He went up to the daughter of the bride, in her mid- 20s, dressed in a very short, backless dress, and he placed his hand on her back. Such a suggestive move."** *Mine did the same thing at a bar once with a girl I knew he used to like before me and it stuck in my head for years. God, they really suck!*

*As for the sex thing, my whole connection was the sex thing and, to this day, it's hard to kick the thought out when it pops in. Only time will heal that wound, I guess, but I agree it's a hard one. It's the hook from hell that many of us can't disconnect from and that's what they count on so that they can hoover weeks, months, and maybe even years from now and we'll still be thinking about it. I assume that the ones that use sex as a hook and are well-practiced at the art will continue to use it until they're too old to get it up. The porn...well, I think that probably comes and goes with the opportunity (and it's always more fun to have that obsession when you have a girlfriend who's bothered by it so they may wait for that...it's part of the triangulation tactic for making a victim actually jealous of it, thus provoking her codependency). Remember...NOTHING...not the sex, not the porn, not the cell phone in the bathroom game, not the suggestive hand touch on another girl's back...NOTHING a narcissist EVER does is without motive. Ever. So, without someone around who will actually get hurt by it (which, after all, is the fun of it!), he may not do any of those things at all until a situation warrants it. Now, the drinking...that may be slightly different story because it is, after all, a self-medication tactic that just may help him forget (for a minute) what an empty shell of a man he really is.*

*Keep doing what you're doing ....except, that is, for the FB peeps which will only hold you back (I know you know that so I won't lecture:) ). I have a feeling you're going to be just fine. And, if you haven't, read that book because it will help you get through the hardest phases!*

# Chapter IX:
## The Intention Factor

The difference between No Contact and a Silent Treatment is the intention of the outcome - and no one knows this better than a narcissistic partner.

About four years ago, out of the clear blue and smack dab in the middle of my narcissistic relationship nightmare, I got real strong and went No Contact on my ex before he had a chance to go silent on me. It was highly unusual behavior on my part and a shocker to both of us since it was he who typically called the communication shots. And I held on tight for quite a few weeks until his incessant pounding on my apartment door caused me to open it, letting the evil in once again for another round.

As some point before I gave in, I had even scribbled the words "No Contact" on the dry erase board that hung on the wall behind my desk as a reminder/affirmation, I suppose, of what I was supposed to be doing. And, for whatever reason, after I let the demon back in, I neglected to erase the reminder, deliberately and perhaps purposely opening myself up to ridicule and arguments as to my intention with the silence. For several weeks, there I sat and there he sat and there sat those words – *No Contact* – looming on the wall behind me like the elephant in the room and neither of us said a word.

Then, one day, I happened to turn around to write a date on the board and noticed that the narcissist had made a change – albeit when I wasn't looking - to my scribbled affirmation. With a black marker, he had drawn an angled line through the word *No* in *No Contact* and written *Mo* above it so that it now read *Mo Contact* (as in slang for MORE Contact, of course). I have to admit, I thought it was pretty funny then and I think it's pretty funny even now. I left that "correction" up on that dry erase board for months after and, again, it loomed behind me and we never said a word.

How can we possibly expect the narcissist take No Contact seriously if we don't take it seriously enough to stick to it? We can't. To a narcissist, there's absolutely no difference between a silent treatment and a little dose of no contact and, hell, he knows *all about* the dynamics of a silent treatment. Specifically, he knows that a silent treatment doesn't last forever and, therefore, the same rule must apply to the No Contact Rule. This is how he thinks when we don't show him differently...when we don't mean what we say and say what we mean.

Most narcissist victims, even as painful as it is, *do* understand that implementing No Contact is and always will be the only effective means to gaining back our sanity. So, we spend a lot of time talking about it and trying to create new and better ways to maintain it so that we don't do exactly what the narcissist thinks we're going to do – give in. It's all about the intention going in. When you make a decision to go No Contact, you have to first ask yourself "Am I going No Contact, or am I giving him the Silent Treatment?" because silent treatments, as we know, are temporary. A silent treatment – aside from being cruel and unusual (and the narcissist's favorite "punishment") - is intended to prove a point (oh… how well we know *that*!) or to teach a lesson or to buy time to be a cheating bastard or whatever. It's nothing more than a dreadful narcissistic tactic intended to HURT. The intention of No Contact should be nothing other than to END IT. Sure, it would be nice if No Contact HURT the narcissist but this is doubtful. Narcissistic injury is not the same as the gut-wrenching feeling we get when we're discarded. It's not even close. Going NC actually gives us the last word - finally! NC, whether we know it or not, is the closure from the narcissist we've been looking for.

I was very guilty of this myself (as shown in my Mo Contact anecdote)…of not taking the No Contact Rule seriously…of not going into it with the appropriate intention. I'm certain that I went "no contact" more than once to get the narcissist's attention. **This is wrong.** We can't seriously implement No Contact yet still look at/allow texts, emails, Facebook contact, or continue to drive-by, etc. If the intention is really to END IT…to go No Contact…then all of that must stop. Numbers must be blocked or changed, emails deleted, Facebook accounts blocked or, better yet, deactivated. We can't have it both ways.

The difference between No Contact and a Silent Treatment is the intention of the outcome.

Now, I'm not saying any of this is easy because it certainly *is not.* And I'm not saying that if you go No Contact and fall off the wagon that you can't get up and instantly start over because you *can* (and you *must*). And I'm not saying that if you fall off the wagon, then your intention was disingenuous because that's not necessarily true. I'd much rather that you *intend* to end it and mess up than go into the plan with the intention of playing the same old game with the narcissist – only in reverse. It's a game we'll never win.

Everything we do in life should be done with an intention. For anyone who believes (as I do) in Universal concepts such as the Law of Attraction, then you know what I'm talking about. The Universe *knows* your true intention and will give to you accordingly and the narcissist, believe it or not, is keenly aware of your true intentions as well. If you really want him to go away, go No Contact with the right intention and he eventually will [NOTE: the exception, of course, would be a co-parenting situation where complete NC is often impossible]. As long as we *start* with the right intention, even if mistakes are made, I believe we will eventually get what we really want (albeit not as quickly). When we enter NC with the intention for it to be temporary, the game continues, we remain the narcissist's puppet, and time continues to be wasted.

It's all up to you how you handle your suffering at the hands of the N and letting go of anything is never easy. It's a complex situation that calls for us to be aware of our intentions (and boundaries) more than ever. Let's be honest with ourselves and with each other no matter how hard or how painful it gets. And if we feel confused, there's always someone on the team who understands. We are, after all, in this together.

Baby steps, everyone, and we can all hold hands.

**From: Mary**

*It's been two weeks since my N invoked the silent treatment. I asked him to return my door keeps because I found out he is seeing someone else and I got tired of the lies. When I asked for the keys he was shocked and said, "I beet your pardon." I restated I want my keys back and he stated he was not leaving the house that day to dropped them off, then asked if he could mail them to me??? I wonder why he did not want to face me to hand over the keys. I called him today twice and he is not picking up. Can someone explain to me why you he needs keys when he is not using them and when I told him I am done — why not just hand over the keys and move on,*

**From: Me**

*He's just doing what narcissist's do...controlling the situation and keeping you in the chaos. You can fix it once and for all by changing the locks, blocking his number, ceasing to call him anymore ever. If he doesn't care about you or your history together (which he doesn't), then why should he care about returning the keys to you just because you want him to. He's a jerk and jerks do not cooperate. He WANTS you to keep calling and demanding the keys. Why? SO HE CAN IGNORE YOU. And he also would like to hold onto the keys just in case his new victim does something he doesn't like and he needs a place to hang out. Stop giving him the satisfaction of either/or!!! Change the locks, make it so he CAN'T call you even if he wanted to and you take back the control. You don't have to text him or tell him because he doesn't deserve an explanation. OR, if you do want to sort of get the last word, STOP calling him but DO send him a short text saying something QUICK & SIMPLE like "Forget the keys. Locks are changed. I'll mail YOU your things". THEN INSTANTLY BLOCK HIM OR CHANGE YOUR NUMBER. DO NOT WAIT FOR A RESPONSE BECAUSE THAT IS SHOULD NOT BE THE INTENT. Then, pack up his shit and send it or have a friend help you put it out by the curb. By demanding that he "face you" when he drops off the keys is just dragging out the inevitable. You know he is NEVER going to change or see that he is a complete dick so why waste any more energy on this dude than you already have?*

*Take charge of an easily fixable situation and move on to a happy life, girl!!*

# Chapter: X:
## *Avoiding Triggers*

Once you've decided to go No Contact, avoiding the triggers that could cause you to backslide obviously becomes very important. For each of us, although some triggers may be unique to the relationship, most of the triggers will be exactly the same. Hence, the reason for my making the list in this section.

What makes No Contact triggers different than, say, Silent Treatment or Discard triggers is that they will be far more intense than ever before and they will start coming rapid fire. You see, as I said before, when you commit to going NC, you are in total control – and we, as victims of narcissist abuse, are, as a rule, not very good at being in control. Sure, we may fight to gain control at certain times with the N but the truth is that we'd rather give in than pull out because it's much easier on us men tally. And, besides, the narcissist is always so much happier and nicer to us when he feels in charge of the situation…when he feels that we've been punished enough for our misdeeds and  then allows things to go back to temporarily semi-normalcy. When we're *not* in control in our relationship with the N, the sexual tension is at its highest and we cherish this to no end because sex is the *only* connection that we actually have with this person that makes us feel special in an y way.

Yes, we were certainly willing to give up all of the control in our relationship just to have good sex and crumbs of attention. Sad but true. So, now that we've taken control and committed to cutting off all communications with this person so that we can work on our much-needed recovery, whatever triggers in the past that caused  us to backslide or start groveling or apologize for things we didn't even do are going to start coming at us like emotional sucker punches. I'm telling you this because I want you to be aware and be ready. Get your avenues of support in order so that you can deflect and intercept these punches. Allow no room for incoming pain. Believe me, the pain you will probably feel *inside* – at least in the beginning – will keep you plenty busy.

1. **You need "closure".**  The truth is..*no you don't*. First of all, closure is a made up word that means nothing in real life. It doesn't exist. Second of all, when your ex-partner is a narcissist, he's going to make damn sure that you don't feel anything even close to what you  imagine closure feels like. What you really want is the last word so that you feel in control. A narcissist will never give you the last word about anything and you already know this. The fact that you've gone No Contact *is* your closure and it *is* the last word (by being no word at all!). Going No Contact immediately puts you in the drivers seat, allowing you to take control – finally – of your own life.

2. **You miss the sex.** I understand this all too well because it was the only thing I missed (and sometimes *still* miss) from my

relationship. However, just like everything else that happened in the relationship, the sex was a lie. Sure, you both enjoyed it and perhaps this was the only time that you felt he really cared about you. But the connection that *you* felt certainly was not the connection *he* felt and now , probably as you read this, he is making someone else feel that very same fake connection. It's what he does and it's who he is. Don't let your body get in the way of your head when your NC. If you feel horny, take a shower, do what you have to do, but do not give in to the urge to be a buddy fuck. Believe me, the pain and sadness you feel now will only intensify and you will be right back where you started.

3. **You forgot to tell him something**. No you didn't. There isn't a single thing you need to tell him that he deserves to hear. Let it go.

4. **Everything reminds you of him**. Okay, so what are you reminded of? The abuse? A good time during the vacation you paid for? The few times that you actually shared a real laugh? It was all fake, my friend. Turn the radio off. Refrain from playing the same sad songs over and over. Take his pictures down. Take off the bracelet he gave you during the love-bombing stage. Don't let material things become triggers. This is about your life.

5. **He still has his stuff at your house**. Of course, he does. Narcissists love to leave things behind so that they can come back without a care in the world and watch you squirm while they casually walk away. Pack his shit up in a box and send it UPS. Resist the urge to send him an angry text telling him to come and

get it. If you do, he won't respond anyway (to show you he's still in control) and then you're back at square one. And even if he did respond to say he'd come by, chances are he'll never show up and the cycle of waiting will begin once again. Again, stuff it all in a box (without a note from you) and send it UPS.

6. **You still have stuff at his house**. This is a bit trickier because, as victims, we leave things behind for the same reasons. Have a friend that you trust *not* to have a conversation with the man collect it for you or, better yet, consider it a loss and let it go. If you know in advance that you are going to go NC, casually take the items home beforehand.

7. **You need a ride or have a flat tire**. Call a friend. Get roadside service. Chances are he'd bitch about having to come and help you anyway. Mine never came for me at all. And, whatever you do, please do not *create* emergencies as an excuse to call or text him. Be aware and *beware* of this trigger because it can happen in a split second. The littlest thing can become an emergency.

8. **He owes you money**. This is a hard one because there's nothing worse than feeling not only that has your heart been broken by betrayal but that your bank account has been wiped out as well. My feeling on this – and I counsel with this advice as well – is to let it go and here's why: *he's never going to pay you anyway*. But letting it go doesn't mean that you can use the money owed as an excuse to contact him down the road because that would defeat the purpose. So, unless it's a ridiculous amount of money, he's a

millionaire, and you have a lawyer (and the energy to put yourself through *that)*, please cut the financial ties, implement No Contact, and begin your recovery.

9. **You have mutual friends.** Cut the ties that bind. It will hurt less than you think because seeing these people is only going to be hurtful. So, please, just back away quietly and avoid situations where you have to see or engage with them in any way – at least for awhile.

10. **A friend calls to tell you that she saw him on Facebook bragging about a new girl.** This person is *not* your friend. If you absolutely must stay friends with those people that know him as well, you must make it clear that you do not want to talk about him or hear about anything he's doing. Those people that are true friends will abide by your wishes and find other things to talk about. Those that aren't will fall away on their own and if they do continue to call to spread the gossip, hang up, block them, and put their name on the No Contact list.

11. **You miss his family.** No you don't. To cut these particular ties is crucial to a successful run with No Contact. (*See Chapter XII*)

12. **You drank too much.** Avoid the party-rebound method of dealing with your end of No Contact at least for at least six months to a year. Alcohol and NC do not mix well and I'm sure you know this. While a night out with the girls or even just one girlfriend might *sound* like a much-needed steam-releaser, we both know exactly what will happen after a few drinks. You will become a

drink-dialing fool and all your NC efforts will be for naught. Avoid it from happening completely and just don't go.

**13. You had sex with someone else and now you *really* miss him.** I tried this several times over thirteen years and I discuss it at length in both of my books. When I was younger, it used to work but, then again, those guys weren't narcissists and it was much, much easier to get over the break-up. As I got older and became more attached to the sexual aspect of my relationship with the N, the harder it was to find that same feeling with someone else. I actually became a lot like the N, disappearing after a date with a really nice guy and causing the poor dude to wonder what the hell happened. It was wrong of me to do that, it really was. The ties we have to the N are seeped in codependency and in order to recover, we simply must put some distance between ourselves and any type of physical relationship.

*From: Maggie*

*It was on Sunday that I ran across your website after doing a Google search for Narcissists and BPD. I got your ebook and spent the night reading it...just like you said, it was like something I would have written because the stories are so similar...so many "aha!" moments (well, more like lightning bolt moments for me). I found myself stomping my foot and yelling "Yes!" at all the revelations as they were just like mine! I am SO relieved to be able to put a name to this madness that I've been experiencing for the last 2 years, that I'm not "losing it", which is what I originally thought. I wish I could say I'm surprised that so many others have also experienced this. Ours is a narcissistic society to begin with, but these asses take it to a whole sickening other level.*

*I'm a little ashamed to admit that I broke NC after 2 weeks. This was not my first time doing NC but it was my longest. Usually I'd do it and we'd go no longer than 3 days, at which time he'd send a corny text or two and I'd respond and then – as we all know – back to Square One. Before this last NC, we had a fairly decent conversation. - and then nothing. The NC was basically my not saying anything until he said something first. Two whole weeks. I wonder, had I not sent a "hello", how long would it have been? That's what I'm kind of confused on. I don't know whether to classify it as a NC (because I didn't reach out) or a Silent Treatment (because HE didn't reach out). When I broke NC two days ago, we only exchanged a few words. He didn't act an ass, but he didn't have very much to say. Not even the usual "Where have you been?" I haven't heard anything since Monday. I remember reading something about "final discard" and I wonder if this is what's going on right now.*

*Knowing this person like I do (and I use the word "person" loosely), he'll almost certainly turn up again. He's done this kind of stupid shit off and on since 1991. Time is irrelevant to him (seems like I read that this is yet another N quirk)...he could go a couple of years...just to be able to say, "wow, I haven't seen you in two years!" It's crazy. He waited until 2011 to contact me thru FB although we both had been there since like, 2009. I think with him it's this "how long can I stay in her life" type game. He's already boasted, "I know you. I know what you like." Which essentially is saying to me, "I have you where I want you." It's like I can't make myself forget him, and it's infuriating! I had a really bad evening yesterday. I felt like a corpse — barely moving and couldn't even get a complete sentence out. My son, who works at night, came and could tell something was really wrong because we normally talk about his day before going to bed. Last night I just sat, staring into space and not talking. All I could manage to say was "tired", because I don't want anyone around me to know. I was taken for a fool, and it's beyond embarrassing. Some of his enablers would probably think I had this coming, as he proceeded to make me out to be the biggest bitch who ever lived when I dumped him shortly after I went to college. He told our story to anybody who'd listen, and now there are enough people who define me by that long-ago incident (which he highly exaggerated to make himself out as the ultimate victim) to fill a small town. Some of these folks I've never even met, believe it or not.*

*The way this N's tries to turn this shit back around on me makes me want to grab an aluminum bat and go to his house and commence to beating. Whenever I bring up the fact that the most recent situation (affair) I had with him was NOT what I had in mind, he goes back to, "Well, the way you were hugging and kissing on me, you wanted to go to that room as much as I did." But that's not entirely true: I wanted our initial meeting (after having gone 20 years without having seen or heard from each other) to be in a public spot, over lunch or coffee or something. I already knew what would happen if we met in private...but he has said over and again that NO, he wasn't going to meet in public b/c people might see...I didn't know what he had going on (probably other NS all over the place) so I agreed to meet him in private...and it resulted in this big, ugly, wide-open can of worms. He had the whole damn scenario planned from the beginning. I tried to justify it by telling myself he was unhappy at home and was in the process of leaving. But no—during one argument he flat out said, "I NEVER told you I was unhappy at home. I NEVER said that." I asked, "Why? Why'd you take me through all this (I was away from my family during Christmas 2011 because I got so fed up with both him and my husband that I downed a whole bottle of prescription migraine meds and alcohol and ended up in the hospital) if it meant nothing to you?" His reply: "I was just being a man." During the whole conversation he was whining and on the verge of tears, begging me to "just stop, just leave me alone"...like he was five years old. I was at work during this conversation and had to hang up and run to the bathroom, I got so sick. My family was separated that Christmas; as far as I know his was totally unaffected. I never received an apology. Nothing. The unfairness of it feels like a punch in the stomach, even to this very day.*

*It was shortly after this past New Years (after I got tired of being treated like an object, which has been the only way he wanted to relate to me after the Christmas fallout of 2011...I went from being the precious "one who got away", his "hero" to a thing to play with) that I threatened to tell his wife. This is when he uttered the famous: "Ma'am, you're harassing me; I'm calling the cops. I am grown! What do you want from me?" This is also when he proceeded to tell me about some other instances where he'd had to call the cops on some other "crazy" women in the past. I guess that explains why he has 21 guns (all of which he sent me pics of, during what I believe was his Devaluation phase). I suppose, in his twisted mind, I'm just supposed to be ok with it all, let him come in and out of my life for the rest of my life at will, sneak around with him until he gets ready to seek new NS, lather, rinse, repeat. Be on "standby" and just "take it to my grave" (these are all things he has said, when referencing females who just faded into the background once he was through with them). I was the first he'd ever been with, which means I have suffered far too long (longer than any of the others) behind this jackass NUTJOB to just go off gently into the night. So I feel it's only fitting for me to be the one to shut his evil ass down. Don't know how I'm gonna do it yet, but I do know that it has to be done safely and with grace. He's not worth my freedom...but so help me, nothing would give me more satisfaction right now than to see him with his balls caught in a vice (both literally AND figuratively).*

**From: Me**

*Thank you for reading my book and I knew you'd be able to relate! The point is this: what does the silence mean to YOU? You* can go No Contact without even discussing it with him, you know. Going No Contact isn't about HIM at all, it's about YOU and saving YOUR life from his bullshit. He can be in the middle of subjecting YOU to a silent treatment and, in a split second, you can change it to you going No Contact on HIM just by saying to yourself "This isn't a silent treatment, this is NO CONTACT!!" Do you understand what I mean? Again, it depends on you and YOUR intention, not HIS. We already KNOW what HIS intention is. My article discusses all this and will definitely provide you with more clarity on this.

All of the behaviors you describe match all those in my books, right, and therefore you know what you are dealing with. Now, it all boils down to what you want to deal with in your life. All this crap he's pulling – the back and forth, the threats – nothing is going to change – ever. And you will never get closure so forget about that. I have articles on my site about that as well. And sending you threats relative to guns and sending you PICTURES of all these guns is an ILLEGAL THREAT that he could go to fucking jail for and don't you erase any of it because there may come a time that you'll need to report it. I'm serious about that. Think about the audacity of HIM threatening to call the cops on YOU at the same time that he's sending you threatening pictures of guns "that he knows how to use"!!!!!! Even if he showed back up today, you can't forget that he has done that!! This is so typically narcissist, it's ridiculous. Tonya, the Devaluation stage started long before those pictures – it's been going on forever...think *hard. For as long as it's been bad, he's been in the process of devaluing you. The fact that he doesn't want to really talk right now is pretty much the Discard....but who cares? Turn it around in your mind. You must re-establish NC right now in your own mind, girl.*

*Be very careful about wanting to get even because HIS revenge on YOUR revenge will be 100 times worse. He will cross boundaries you didn't even know you had to destroy you. And he will cross boundaries that you wouldn't even THINK of crossing. Put nothing past him....please heed my warning. Revenge never got me anywhere and, believe me, I tried. Half of what I went through isn't even IN my books.*

*Bottom line.....are you willing to put up with "fairly decent conversations" every once in awhile as the best you're going to get from this guy? You are going to have to let so many things go in order to be able to have peace. I know it's hard, believe me, but whether this is a silent treatment or no contact, it's still a silence and you need to have Silence Appreciation and work on this time to get stronger. I have an article series about that on this site and also it's in my second book. That's how I got stronger. I practiced on getting better by using the silences....and when he finally walked away...the FINAL DISCARD...I let it happen. Sure, I was sad but I never shed a tear. I wrote a book instead. And here I am now. It can and WILL happen for you too if you let it.:)*

# Chapter XI:
## No-Reaction Strategies

If you remember nothing from this book or from any of the books I have written, at least remember this: *a narcissist only returns again and again to ensure that you never move on from the pain he has caused you*. And that is the *only* reason, my friends.

No Contact works because it places a special kind of distance between the victim partner and the N that can not be bridged because it's basically against the rules. Even though we've either broken up with or been dumped by this person hundreds of time throughout the relationship, the truth is that we never gave the "distance factor" the respect and consideration that it deserved. We didn't take it seriously. Subconsciously, we'd always leave that revolving door ajar *just enough* so that the N could squeeze in and out whenever he liked. Maybe this isn't something that we'd admit to in the moment but we sure as hell have all done it! Because the narcissist knows this, he's never really worried about "breaking up" or going silent or disappearing or even of *you* telling *him* to fuck off for any length of time. He loves the fact that the door is always open because it means he can keep his finger on the relationship reset button for whenever the mood strikes or his newest target misbehaves. At that point, it's all about getting you to react to something – *anything* - because any reaction (negative or positive) serves as successful narcissistic supply.

No Contact is intended to put an end to all of this bullshit because NC is a ***no-reaction strategy***. If you commit to having no reaction to anything he does, there is no way that the narcissist can ever beat you at your own game. There simply is no way he can ever weasel his way back. Unfortunately, this is the challenge of No Contact because it's a sad and frustrating fact that a narcissist will – without fail and sooner or later – attempt to return to the scene of a crime to ensure that his narcissistic supply is still pining for him. This return, of course, is known as a *hoover* and if there's one thing a narcissist learns to perfect in life, it's the art of hovering.

As we know, the typical *hoover* usually follows a silent treatment (i.e. break-up in disguise) and comes long after the victim has been completely devastated by the silence. The narcissist may **1)** come back *full-on* by just showing up, picking up right where he left off and thus laying the groundwork for the next discard which will be more crippling to the victim than all the ones before, or **2)** not being quite finished with his newest target, he hoovers with a simple and sporadic text specifically intended to be more of a warning or *warm-up* to get you feeling anxious, confused, and maybe even quietly excited about his possible return. The point is..*it's all a crock of shit to get a response from you so that communication is initiated and he can worm his way back into your life.* How fast and furious the hoovering becomes is based solely on your response to the first few. This is why it is imperative that you block this person from reaching you at all costs.

A *hoover* will happen whenever the narcissist chooses and typically not until he's been gone just slightly longer than the time before. By staying away just a tad longer than the time before, the narcissist conditions his victim to not only *expect him* to come back *eventually* but also to expect him to come back at a *much later date*. In doing this, the narcissist gets more play time in the interim. Again, this is all part of the narcissist's control/validate tactic which I discussed in *Chapter II* and it's all a part of the process of managing down your expectations.

The narcissist's intention, above all else, is to always make sure that you're in the queue, ready and waiting alongside all the others (and there are *always* others). It's a sick game of cat and mouse that will steal *years* from your life if you allow it. For this reason alone, no contact must be enforced in order to succeed in your recovery. No Contact is the key to escaping the narcissist's plan for you and the only opportunity you'll ever have for breaking the codependency to hope that he *counts on you to cling to* while he is gone. Remember, the narcissist is *never* worried about what you're doing while he's gone or that you've found a better love because he's conditioned you to act a certain way. He's *counting on it* based on how he's seen you react either to his leaving or to his returning.

*It's time to ignore the signs of hoovering.* Even if you notice subtle signs of the narcissist's return, ignore them and go on with your life. No one has a right to come and go in your life and manipulate your emotions. In addition, we know for a fact that the narcissist's plan is *always* to make the next discard even more painful than the one before. *Say "no more" and mean it!*

It is the hoovering – this preferred narcissistic tactic of our toxic insignificant other – that invariably lures us back into the abyss for another round of cat and mouse. It is the hoovering that gets the best of us – more often than not – and makes it nearly impossible for us to put an end to the narcissistic nonsense.

### From: Katie

*I have not slept or eaten all weekend. I have no idea how I will get through today. The betrayal is unbearable. The worst thing is his lack of remorse. When I showed him what I'd found out, he just attacked me back about something ridiculous. And this time last week he was in my bed! In fact, our last conversation was just last Friday...and he was up on the dating website by Saturday morning. His response was to suggest he had only been on there since we split. . What - within 12 hours? Surely you would think he'd be embarrassed that he'd been busted – but no, nothing!*

*He just attacked back when he had clearly done something unforgivable. Even his profile on there was a lie.... He drives a car (doesn't have a license I can tell you) and he put he has a masters degree..... He has not one qualification. I feel sick... Picturing him with other women.... I cannot get those thoughts out of my head. Do you think he will do the same to there women? I am so scared he will go on to have a loving perfect relationship whilst I remain single and damaged.*

*The website he was on was free and well known to end in one night stands.... I am crying now. Do you think he will attempt to return again?*

*Surely he would not dare after this? I will NEVER forgive him this time EVER Have to go to work now, cannot bear it*

**From: Me**

   *I know you are hurting but in your pain, you are losing sight of the big picture. David is a textbook narcissist. He is exactly the same as all the other narcissists. He is going to keep doing what narcissists do. It is never going to change. This is as good as its ever going to get. Life is a game to David and he feels nothing. What has happened here is that David knows you are on to him. Because of this, he no longer has the patience to keep up the facade for any length of time. I talk about this in the book. Me and my ex would stay in bed all weekend, having a wonderful time, and within a few hours of his leaving, all hell had broken loose over something as if the earlier part of the day had never happened. I would beg him..."Why??? But everything was good! We had such a great day!" It means nothing to a narcissist. In fact, last weekend, while you and David were in bed, he was already planning his next escape via the Snapchat excuse or whatever. NORMAL PEOPLE DO NOT ACT THIS WAY. HE IS NOT AND NEVER WILL BE NORMAL. Everything a narcissist does and says is a Lie.*

   **Do you think he will do the same to other women?** *Yes, of course he will eventually because he is incapable of having a normal relationship. As soon as any relationship he has demands that he act in a normal manner, he'll flee to the next source of supply. But look at what he's doing (and again I talk about this in the book)...he's reinventing himself online (a narcissist's favorite playground because he* *gets to LIE and be whoever he wants). What do you think is going to happen if he meets up with one of these women? How long do you think it will take for them to figure out he's a big fat sociopathic liar??? About three minutes!!! Don't even worry about it. Trust me, he's an idiot and he's made himself out to be something that he has NO INTENTION of trying to be. Why? BECAUSE IT'S ALL A GAME. If he's incapable of loving YOU, how could he possibly love anyone else?? He doesn't have the vaguest idea what the word "love" means. All he knows is that if he pretends to love someone who has something he wants, he might get it.*

***Do you think he will attempt to return again?*** *Maybe but he knows you are on to him so he may not. When my ex finally left, the scenario played out in the exact same manner. When they know, they know. And the entire history is erased because it never mattered in the first place.*

*Try to look at it this way:* ***suppose you discovered that David was a serial killer. Would you cry for long? Or even AT ALL??*** *No! There's no difference! David is NOT a good person whether he's killing people or breaking hearts. It's all the same. The mindset is the same. Narcissists just don't care. YOU have a chance at a normal life. Sister, at some point we have to cut our losses and move on. You only have ONE LIFE. If it ended tomorrow, this debacle with Martin would be your legacy! I had to really look at that to get it but when I did, I vowed it would NOT be my legacy. No fucking way!*

*You're going to be okay, girlfriend. You really are going to be okay. Please keep reading...my books...the articles on this website...articles on other sites....the more you read, the MADDER you're going to get.*

*Get rid of the sad and get mad. I'm not going to say you shouldn't be sad because of course your are. But it's not like this is the first time this has happened. He's done this to you 100's of times. The bad times and the level of betrayal outweigh any good memory we ever had of these fuckers. Don't worry about what he's doing because it just doesn't matter. He's going to do what he does no matter WHAT you do so you might as well do something else besides what you're doing right now. It's okay, girl. Breathe. And write anytime.*

### 

**From: Darianne**

*I've recently been busy reading & researching NPD. It's so creepy - your book/website could have been written by me about my Narcissist! After splitting 6 months ago with this guy, I've experienced above all else the narcissist's rage and it's absolutely horrendous, Nothing but verbally abusive phone calls that have left me shaken, anxious & unable to sleep/concentrate.*

*I decided to enforce the NC rule about 2.5 months ago following a particularly horrible conversation. I had assumed he'd get the message loud & clear (I mean, he's an intelligent guy right?) WRONG!*

*On my birthday, I received a delivery from Fed Ex and it was from him. Always expect the unexpected, everyone, because it wasn't a card, gift or an attempt to win me back. Oh no! It was a black & white canvas print of me in my underwear that I'd asked back for months ago. He was trying to not only prompt a reaction but to show me how I'd been disgraced. I don't for one minute think that receiving this on my birthday was a coincidence. He times it perfectly!*

*Following this delivery, I received a call from an Anonymous ID (I've blocked his number) with someone listening in silence and then hanging up after 10 seconds. Then, my Apple account was hacked & the password re-set...both events happening within 10 minutes of one another.*

*And this week, while I've been on holiday trying to escape the nightmare, guess what?! More contact! I'm not sure how he found out I was away but so far I've received 2 calls, a voicemail, a message on WhatsApp (now blocked), and 2 emails. The initial contact concerned a wedding we've both been invited to. I'd previously told him I'd be going so now he's was checking on that (yeah, right). The email was blunt but not rude, the WhatsApp message apologized for interrupting my holiday, and then voicemail said he needed to speak to me urgently.*

*I've managed to stay strong & not respond but its soooo fucking hard!*

*Today I received an email bright and early at 6am which read "Your friends with Kate?? WTF is going on with you?" To explain, Kate is an ex-girlfriend of his who he'd painted out to be a complete psycho. In reality, she's a lovely girl who had a psychological breakdown after he discarded her. Makes sense to me!!! We've become friends & managed to support one another. Thankfully, she has now moved on & has a great BF.*

*My point here is that a narcissist will try ANYTHING to prompt a reaction. You can block numbers, change numbers, move 100 miles away probably and they'll ALWAYS find a way to get to you. No Contact is hard but absolutely necessary and I'm hoping a year on from now it continues to become easier to cope with. I love the fact it's our ONLY way of getting back at them & it sure does work!*

**From: Me**

*Thank you so much for writing because I get your message loud and clear...... You have the solution, girl, and you just keep doing what you're doing because, as hard as it is, you are doing everything right!*

*It's all about getting a REACTION and he sure has tried, hasn't he? One reaction is all it takes to put a narcissist back in the driver's seat in his twisted mind. Why give him that? You are so right to turn to your support group of friends as a way to get around it. And for those who don't have that, come to websites like this one and others where there's a world of virtual friends waiting to help. Wonderful advice....*

*###*

**From: Karen**

*I felt the need to write tonight...I'm going to see a therapist on this Friday because I feel like a mixed up bag of crap. As I was writing things down to discuss with her, I flipped to some things I was writing in my journal about things I've noticed that wasn't right about him. I had 12 things at the time, but believe me by the time the relationship was over there were plenty more. I started crying asking myself "why, why didn't I leave him then?" He was ALWAYS disappearing or not* answering the phone, but would turn around and tell me that I was controlling and a drama queen. I would ask him to explain how I was both, but he never could give me any reason.

I thought about a particular event one evening when I spent the night over to his home. This night we did not have sex or anything and because of his snoring, he slept on the couch and I slept in the bed. When I starting making up the bed, I found a hair pen in the bed...I walked in the living room and slammed it on the table and replied I found a hair pen in the bed. This bitch got fuming mad and was like, "don't start that shit Lisa, that's probably (the grand daughter's name) or YOUR hair pen." I was like I don't wear hair styles that require hair pens and the grand daughter hadn't been over. He went on to say that he doesn't even sleep in the bed and he doesn't know how it got there, etc. I was sooooo hurt, but guess what, I started thinking did I have a hair pen in my head??? crazy huh? this is why I'm going to see a therapist cause I'm wondering how in the hell was I so gullible. I'm like SOOOO angry with myself. Then this bitch didn't even have the nerves to change the damn sheets, cause if he had the hair pen wouldn't have been there. Right now I want revenge on him soooo bad, but the Lord said vengeance is his. I gotta get through this...

**From: Me**

Come on....are you sure you weren't seeing my boyfriend??? LOLOL Sounds so frigging familiar. I, too, found something in my ex's bed – a broken piece of a bracelet and I did the same thing, demanding answers, and he kicked my ass and threw a livid fit. I call these fits

**distraction reactions** *because they are intended to turn things quickly – and they do. Before I knew it, I was apologizing because – hell – maybe it was my bracelet (it was not, of course!). Either way, I chose to go the easy route rather than face the truth. Just one more thing that I stuck on the backburner....for what? So he could do it again? We all do it and you're not – nor have you ever been – crazy. These guys are very good at what they do or they wouldn't be narcissists.*

*You're in good company, girl. There are literally thousands of us scratching our chin, wondering what the hell happened? It's hard to accept the truth but just know it was never ever you. He's just a monster, plain and simple.*

# Chapter XII:
## Cutting the Ties that Bind

Another reason that a victim may avoid going No Contact or feel the need to break No Contact is the fact that she and the N share mutual friends and/or she happens to be close to a member (or all of the members) of the narcissist's family. I understand that this situation can get tricky but I only have one answer for it: *cut the ties that bind.* Unfortunately, you simply must separate from everything and everyone – at least for awhile – that has anything to do with the guy you're banishing from your life.

Once a person decides to go NC, I believe that having mutual friends causes anxiety because of the nagging feeling we get that we owe these people an explanation. Trust me, you don't. In fact, I prefer that you say absolutely *nothing* to anyone so that you can get to the point where you stop uttering his name immediately. The word will get out in the manner that words *always* get out and you needn't have to say a thing. As soon as you commit to NC, the intention is to become instantly disconnected from the suffering. It's not your concern what he's saying behind your back or how back he's trashing your name. Seriously, it's not. Unless he's jeopardizing your job by calling your boss, anything he has to say from this moment forward should be of no concern to you. This is how it's supposed to be in theory, anyway!

Relevant to mutual friends, I always found this issue very confusing because it appeared to me that whoever happened to come around had nothing to talk to me about *but* the break-up or what the narcissist was doing or what he *had* been doing all along but, of course, they weren't able to tell me that before. *Yeah, right. Tell me now, bitch.* Just looking into the *eyes* of someone who I knew might be looking into *his* eyes later that day made me want to throw up. Personally, I wasn't interested in the company of certain people suddenly and I felt okay about it. Avoiding them – or at least stepping back so as not to be so readily available for conversation – felt calming to me. We simply *must* break the ties that bind in order to be finally free. Those you sincerely cared about *you* during the friendship will understand and be there for you whenever you're ready. A chosen few will automatically know that speaking non-stop about the N or inadvertently slipping a story about him and his new girl into the conversation is a no-no. They will hear you pain and anguish loud and clear and they will abide by your wishes....if they are truly friends, that is. And if they don't....if they even one time hurt your feelings or make you cry over a verbal mess-up, then they weren't your friends to begin with. *Fuck 'em in that case!*

The same rules apply to family members of the narcissist whom you may have felt close to. This in and of itself would be out of the norm since most victims are kept separated from the narcissist's family by the narcissist himself for obvious reasons. After all, keeping you close to the family would mean that he felt that you were *like* family and we know *that's* not true. Since my ex would pack up and move to his mom's with every disappearance, he made damn sure that I felt unwelcome in that house, whereby providing him assurance that I wouldn't come pounding on the door. Late night drive-bys through the cul-de-sac to check for his car was as close as I ever got to *that* house, believe me. The truth of the matter is that the N is blood and you're not and even though his sister and/or the mom might swear up and down that they *know* he's a creep and that everyone's on your side, it's a lie – albeit, a *well-intentioned* lie, perhaps, but a lie nonetheless. If this is an issue, you'll have to let family members go forever and, once you do, you will feel an even bigger sense of freedom and separation from the drama.

Please understand that staying away from the ordinary masses as you attempt to implement No Contact is the best thing you can do. This doesn't mean you have to become a recluse...it just means that you have to create distance between yourself and anything/anyone that could be a trigger for disaster until you're better equipped mentally to handle it. I think that, like most women that I talk to, you'll find yourself *wanting* to be alone with your thoughts and your sadness. And, hey, if you've got sisters, a mom, or girlfriends that have always known what the hell was happening, by all means, gather those familiar shoulders around. It's those in your world that know him or are connected to him in any way that you need to avoid. Lay low with those *you* know and you'll be just fine.

**From: Kathleen:**

Just a quick question... if anyone asks me about my ex N, do I say I don't want to talk about him or what went on or is it okay to tell people who ask what he did to me (as in emotional and physical abuse ) and to our two boys? We were together 28 years so there are lots of people who are going to ask me questions as to why suddenly we're not together.

**From: Me**

Okay, if I were you – at least for now – I would cut off the questions real damn quick. While I do understand that a 28-year relationship has an obvious history with and among friends, so frigging what? The less you have to talk about him (and especially to people he knows), the better for you. You don't owe anyone any explanation whatsoever except maybe to say that its over for those who don't know. The way I see it, conversations could go something like this:

*FRIEND: Hey, how are you?? Haven't seen or heard from you. Are you still with XXXX?*

*YOU: No, I'm sure not and I really can't talk about it right now if that's alright. Anyway, how are you doing?*

*FRIEND: Hey, how the hell are ya?*

*YOU: I'm doing good, thanks. What's up with you?*

*FRIEND: Well, I ran into XXXX and he told me it was over between you two. Is that true?? I couldn't believe it.*

**YOU:** *Yup, it finally is. And I'm really not into talking about it at all so lets skip all that. What have you been doing?*

**FRIEND:** *I am SO sorry. It's just that he said -*

YOU: *Nope, don't want to hear it. Really. I don't care what he said. The truth is the truth. So, anyway, what are you doing?*

**FRIEND:** *Well, actually, he wanted me to give you a message and I said I would...*

**YOU:** *Gotta go, talk to ya later. (hang up or walk away)*

**FRIEND:** *Oh my God, I saw XXXX out with some girl! What the hell is going on? What happened?*

**YOU:** *If you saw him out with some girl, then you pretty much know what happened. It's over. And, really, I don't want to talk AT ALL about it so let's change the subject.*

> **REFUSE TO ENGAGE.** *Slowly but surely, you will discover who are your real friends and who aren't. There will be plenty of people who just want to get the scoop and there will be those who will call you JUST TO tell you things that will hurt you. Blow both of these friend-types* off forever. *A true friend will hear that you don't want to talk about it and never mention it again. There's no reason to go into the abuse and all of the stories because most people are just not going to "get it". Why even put yourself through that? Plus, the quieter you are on your end, the more ridiculous his mouth-flapping looks on his end. That's what I did and my ex HATED it. He'd be talkin' all kinds of shit about me, smirking the way he would do, and then say "I suppose you heard*

*that I was a complete asshole right?". When people would respond with, "Actually, dude, she doesn't talk about you at all", he just couldn't figure it out and I'm sure it made him crazy. In the end, he inevitably looked like a big mouth and I just went about my business being nice and quiet.*

*Anyway, I hope you understand what I'm trying to say. Your ex sounds like he's always got plenty to say so, in light of that, I'd want to be looking like the good guy if I were you. There's plenty of time down the road to fill close friends in on the truth but right now, I'd lay real low and refuse to engage in any conversation about him at all. It's just better for you and the children all around that way.*

# Chapter XIII:
## The Co-Parenting Dilemma

The only thing harder than going No Contact with a narcissist is going No Contact with a narcissist who also happens to be your baby daddy/momma. Based on the countless emails and comments that I receive from victims who struggle to co-parent with a narcissistic ex, it's clear to me that there are no easy solutions. In fact, up until I began to write this book, I was starting to fear that perhaps there were *no* solutions but I quickly decided that this simply wasn't acceptable. So, after giving the subject some very careful thought, I came up with a slightly different perspective on this very unique co-parenting scenario. Ultimately, I decided that co-parenting with a narcissistic ex and having a peaceful life *can* happen because it *must* and that the Agony of Defeat typically felt by the victim parent was not insurmountable.

Can a Narcissist love his/her children? This is the big question, of course, and, unfortunately, the answer is no. The truth is that a narcissist can no more love his or her children than he or she can love a partner, friend, family member, or anyone else. I've never seen it happen. I've never read about it happening. I've never heard about it happening. It's just not possible. An N is an N is an N. If history could somehow prove that even the slightest possibility existed that narcissists could, in fact, love their own children, I'd be tempted to think that narcissism perhaps was fixable. But there is no history *anywhere* that shows this...no history, that is, that is based in fact and not in wishful thinking. No, narcissists do not *and can not* love their children anymore than they can love you, the person who cares and suffers for them the most.

Now, having said that, do not be misled into thinking that narcissists do not find their children *useful* under certain circumstances because...*oh yeah*...they most certainly do. In fact, the N who is a combination "ex-partner" and "co-parent" has the luxury of circulating, surviving, and thriving at levels of evil *far beyond* that of the typical narcissistic asshole. The narcissist co-parent is indeed a SuperPower in his own right! Yes, he who holds this coveted position is awarded the type of false entitlements that a single non-parent narcissist only *dreams* about. And for the victim partner who wants to get away, a break-up with this narcissistic superpower too often appears to be a hopeless situation. To implement No Contact on this person only guarantees a *brand new* narcissistic show of chaos that promises to be far more damaging than the first, second, and third. And, this time, it will be the children who get bumped to the top of the N's hit list.

Is it possible to go No Contact with a narcissist co-parent? In many ways, no... at least not in the way that **No Contact** was originally intended. Victims who want/need the torture to stop but still have to deal with co-parenting issues are left to their own devices without a single one of the privileges that many other victims take for granted. As a victim who co-parents, how do you block a phone number, move away, refuse to answer the door, blow off the in-laws, and so forth when there are children involved? You can't. How do you flat out refuse to communicate with a parent that the children (bless their hearts) have been duped into loving? How do you deal with the fact that the narcissist talks shit about you to the kids and you can't even defend yourself (because you choose to do the right thing and stay quiet)?

Because the N, as a parent, is not a normal human, he is, without a doubt, going to use the children as his narcissistic tactic and weapon of choice to cut you to the very bone. Since he clearly has no conscience, dragging the children into the dirt is nothing but a thing and the easiest way to hurt you. The narcissist co-parent will use every excuse in the book pertaining to the children to intrude upon your new life. At some point, he may even try to scare you into submission - either by threatening to call CPS (for no reason at all) or by saying that he won't be bringing the children back. Granted, while the latter scenario isn't likely because the N simply can't be bothered, the thought is nonetheless horrifying since you *know* he will cross all boundaries both in court and out if he thinks its necessary.

Unfortunately, now that you've separated from this person, you will be forced to watch the nightmare that was your relationship played out and directed towards the children. It's likely the narcissistic father will continually make plans with the children and then not show up or even call to cancel. He will promise to call and then conveniently forget. He may even miss holidays altogether, choosing instead to be with his "new" victim family and partner. He will relish the thought that now, even with the relationship being over, he can continue to torture you by torturing the children. And since the children, at least while they're young, tend to love a narcissist parent unconditionally no matter how neglectful and indifferent he/she may be, the N ultimately gets nearly a life time to make sure you are never happy again!

So, what *is* the answer? The answer, first, is to *know* that the relationship between you and the N is over. At this point, despite how he appears to others, you already *know* the type of parent that he *really* is and must proceed to use this information to (for once) serve your own purpose. How much time did the N really spend with the children anyway? Narcissists are historically *not* doting fathers and mothers or even *participating* fathers and mothers. Over and over, I hear stories of narcissistic fathers walking out *just weeks* after a child is born to start a brand new life with someone else. I hear about new mothers being subjected to silent treatments immediately after coming home from the hospital. Silent treatments!! Can you imagine that?? I hear about narcissists who've walked out just *days* before Christmas, leaving a family of little children with not the slightest idea where daddy went. This may not be exactly the case with your ex-N but I bet its close. Narcissists have the amazing ability to be…well…*narcissists* no matter what the surrounding circumstances. Use this knowledge to your advantage. *You* are a good person. *He* is not.

The secret to achieving some level of survivable co-parent No Contact with a narcissist is that you, too, must strive to be a Super-Power! You must develop thicker skin than you ever thought possible so that every nasty comment he throws your way rolls off your back. You must be able to take an emotional beating without anyone around you being the wiser. You must learn to *detach, detach, detach* from the nonsense and *commit, commit, commit* to setting boundaries and making rules of engagement. Communication, if possible, should be limited to text, email, and the sporadic phone call...and it must *only* concern sensible/reasonable issues about the children. And, really, how many of *those* can there be that have to involve the N? Not many.

Do not worry about and/or feed into the enormous amount of trash-talking going on behind your back. In fact, say nothing and simply observe, allowing the N to talk trash about mommy *all day long* if he wants to. Sit quietly on the sidelines while the pathetic narcissist digs his own parental grave – and he *will* dig it because he just can't help himself. Take comfort in the fact that children are strong, resilient, and smart. They *will* grow up one day and see the narcissist parent for what he/she is and *you* will come out the winner. The mask always slips and that's a fact.

From co-parenting with a narcissist, nothing good *ever* comes... *this* we already know so where else can we really go but up? You must believe in your heart that no matter how hurtful the narcissist is or how evil his intention, you are still free! The relationship is *over*. You may now look upon the Narcissist as nothing more than an annoying sperm donor and treat him accordingly. He deserves nothing less, nothing more. For *years*, the narcissist has been methodically managing down your expectations...preparing for this very day....setting the stage for *this* break-up because he *knew* it would come...it *had* to come. The narcissist co-parent counts on the fact that his passive-aggressive conditioning of your responses to his words and behaviors has stuck and that you still fear what he *could* do, *might* do, *will* do. He counts on *his* control in this situation and *your* emotional fragility. The fact that he gets to use the kids against you is just an added bonus!

Turn it around by having *no more fear*. It's time to up the ante. First, if the narcissist has a girlfriend, tell him you want to be communicative with her *about the children*. Now, the N will *hate* this but that's too bad. Normal couples in normal break-ups speak to "the others" all the time. In fact, you should simply refuse to send the kids unless you *at least* get to speak to her on the phone for five detached minutes about Suzie's sort throat. If you show that you're willing and actually *prefer* to communicate with the OW, the N is likely to begin behaving immediately to ensure this never happens – and that's fine too (it's what we want). I'd be willing to bet that, within a short amount of time, the narcissist will begin to back out completely since the fun of making you suffer will have been taken out of the equation. Using this particular communication twist clearly sends a message to the Narcissistic co-parent that says: *I don't care about you anymore.*

Even if it hurts, do it. What you are doing here is basically forcing him into complying with NC unless it is absolutely necessary. Do not allow fear to keep you from being free. You have to let it all go (narcissist included). Do not let your emotions rule your actions. **You can *still* initiate and implement your own version of No Contact with the narcissist co-parent.** You can *still* move on with your life. Chances are high that if you show indifference, detachment, and a refusal to play the game on his terms in any way, the narcissist will do what he has always done and vanish anyway. The children will *still* grow up to be wonderful people. In the end, you – as the co-parenting ex victim – will be stronger than any of us who have embarked on this journey. Don't allow the co-parenting dilemma to become an excuse to stay connected with the N. Know in your heart that your decision to end it with the N despite the fact that you have children together will *always* be the right decision.

# Chapter XIV:
## Postpone & Pretend

When readers who contact me express an inability to get on with life during NC, I understand this completely. I spent many a day curled up in the fetal position, unable to get up and do the most mundane of daily chores and activities. Sometimes I would sob and sob until the sounds of my crying appeared to reverberate throughout the apartment...as if they came from someone else and not this unbelievably sad person that I had become. I understand that this is a very hopeless feeling and so I developed a little game called *Postpone & Pretend* that helped me get through it.

You see, like you, I knew – even amidst all my sadness – that life *has* to go on. We have families and true friends (who won't leave us alone, thank God) and we *have jobs* that we depend on for sheer survival. Look, I know that going NC on the narcissist feels like the end of the world but you have to remember that *your* sadness only exists within a very small part of *your* reality. The truth is that you've got to get up and go to work if nothing else! And, if you have children...well, this goes without saying. Think of how satisfied the narcissist feels simply knowing that the punishment you're subjecting *him* to is making *you* far more miserable than he is. In fact, it's a good bet that he's not miserable at all! So, you've simply got to get up and keep moving.

For me, forcing myself to change my thought process to one that allowed me *to postpone my sadness* for at least 24 hours (to start) was a miracle cure [the "pretend" part is connected to this and I'll explain momentarily]. When we're feeling sorry for ourselves over breaking the ties, the last thing we want to accept is that we will never ever think about him again. Believe it or not, we *want* to suffer for our decision to go NC because it is our suffering that has always somehow kept us connected to the narcissist. As long as we were suffering, there was always that chance for future contact whether we initiated it or he did. The best times of our lives (during the relationship) always and without fail occurred after a hefty bout of suffering on our part. Maybe it was the knock at the door or the make-up sex or the sudden text hoover, or maybe it was simply the thought of the *possibility* of any of that...whatever it is (and it's different for everyone), the truth is that, combined with a good does of mental anguish, the actual event – if it does occur - is about as close to a mental orgasm as we're ever going to get and it feels fucking great. So, my point here is that, as we suffer through No Contact, it's perfectly okay to play head games with ourselves to get us up and out of the bed. Whatever it takes....and for me it was a game of postponing the sadness for at least another day. If I thought that it would be okay for me to suffer *tomorrow*, then somehow I was able to get up and do the things that I needed to do *today*.

You must remember that *you* – along with a whole lot of help from the Master – *trained* your brain to be codependent to this nonsense. And your brain isn't stupid. You brain knows exactly what it should be doing and thinking and it doesn't take long to retrain it back to pre-narcissist sanity. So, when the alarm clock goes off and you feel like dying or when the children are pounding on the bedroom door or the phone starts ringing…when the world starts reminding you very loudly that you have other responsibilities that have nothing to do with memories of the N, simply POSTPONE THE SADNESS FOR 24-HOURS and get the fuck up. Then, the next morning, when the world screams again, POSTPONE FOR ANOTHER DAY and get the fuck up again. Keep doing this day after day after day. It really works, my friend. I'm not saying you're going to leap out of bed with glee to face the day because the likely scenario is that you'll be moping around in slow motion (at least to start) but at least you'll be on your feet.

Now, once you're up and moving around trance-like (which is okay!!), you're going to find yourself smack-dab in the middle of a world that could give two shits about you missing the narcissist. You finally called it quits with that jerk? Thank God for that! easily turns to What the hell are you so sad for? Isn't this what you wanted? even if nobody admits to it. This is where the "pretend" part of my Postpone & Pretend game comes in. Unfortunately, now that you're up and about and not shirking your responsibilities, you have to act, for the most part, as if everything is fine. You must pretend that this day is like any other. You must act "as if" you can live your life without obsessing about what the N is doing. You must remember that this is it and others do not need to suffer because of your grave relationship error – the one you are trying to desperately fix right now while you're postponing and pretending and implementing No Contact.

I promise you, friend, that if you pretend and postpone enough times, you're going to begin to get better fast! You're going to retrain your brain to get a grip. What this little game is all about is living in the moment....in the here and now. You've got to do it. In the here and now...in this very moment, the N is going about his business doing what he always does and he's going to do this whether you are curled up in a fetal position or whether you are up and out, getting on with your life. What you're doing and how you're feeling doesn't make a bit of difference to this person at all. So, knowing this to be true (that he/she is going to do it no matter what!), which do you choose to do – sink or swim? Think about that. No Contact is the right decision.

You have every right to postpone (the suffering) and pretend (to be happy). The Universe will appreciate your efforts to get better and you will be richly rewarded. Eventually, you'll find yourself simply getting up and going forth. You'll discover that, by pretending to be okay, you can actually share a laugh with a friend without feeling as if you forgot something (him). The truth is that No Contact has to happen in order for you to live your life in the manner that you deserve. If it takes a few months of playing a game of postpone and pretend to make it happen, so be it. It worked for me and I know it can – and will – for you as well. It's going to be a challenge but I know you can do it.

### 

As I thought of ways to close this book, I tried to imagine what it would take for me to finally "get it" if I were a reader with a broken heart...someone who was suffering that awful separation anxiety that comes from breaking up with a narcissistic partner. What is it that finally convinces us that taking an action that hurts us to the very core is really the best thing for us and that the reward for our doing it will be three-fold? I thought about it and then I knew.....*proof.* The answer was that it takes proof. There has to be evidence that something is going to work before we go "all in" and risk it all. There has to be proof of a happy ending before we believe. And I have that proof...that evidence...and it is me. I am here to tell you that I am living proof that No Contact can work. I am evidence that breaking up with a narcissist is survivable. And if I can do it, oh so can you....

As I finish this book, I am a little over two and ½ years into the break-up. Without a doubt, it is *you* who has helped *me* to get better and to get on with my life. Because of my books and my blog, I have met and communicated with amazing, wonderful, smart, witty, and compassionate people – and you are one of them. It has been my privilege to help you through recovery and the biggest gift I can give you is the fact that I'm here and happy.

I feel good and I feel strong and I know that life simply continues whether we like it or not. Time really does heal all wounds just like they always told us. But we have to allow time to do its work without resistance. We have to have faith in what we know to be true about this person who has hurt us. Sometimes when things that are broken are proven completely unfixable (and it's not as if we didn't try!), then we have to throw it out, walk away, and let someone else pick up the pieces. Simply put, there comes a time when we have to decide if we really want to live with this anxious feeling forever and ever. I know that it often feels that the anxiety of being apart from this person is far worse than the anxiety we feel when we're together *with* them but this is simply *not true*. Narcissists condition us to feel that way and it's actually very clever. They create our reality and then use it against us at every turn. If we don't take out power back, what in God's name will happen to us? No Contact is our ticket to freedom and, again, I'm here to tell you that the ride is survivable and you, my friend, are going to survive!

So, go forth and be happy! Stick to No Contact and change your life. Do not let the N twist the rules of the game to serve his purpose. Allow no more manipulation because that part of your life is over!! Instead, beat him at his own game by playing by the rules. With all of my heart, I know you can do it!

# ABOUT THE AUTHOR

Zari Ballard is a home-based Freelance Writer/Author (and single mom!) who resides in sunny Tucson, Arizona at the base of the beautiful Catalina Mountains. In 2005, four years after her son's diagnosis with child-onset schizophrenia, Zari set aside the corporate rat race in lieu of a home-based career as a Freelance Writer. A leap of faith that could have gone either way, the choice was meant-to-be and she has never looked back.

Now, motivated by the success of her first book, *When Love Is a Lie*, Zari plans to ride the wave of self-publishing as far as it will take her. Alongside *When Love Is a Lie, Stop Spinning, Start Breathing, & Narcissist Free*, Zari has also published a book about female narcissism entitled *When Evil Is a Pretty Face*. In addition, she will soon launch a memoir about her son's life as well as podcasts related to topics about narcissism. Be sure and stay tuned!

Visit Zari's Blog: **TheNarcissistPersonality.com**

**If you enjoyed this book, please do submit a review to Amazon! It would be most appreciated.**

# BONUS SECTION:
## Special Book Excerpts
### By Zari Ballard


#### #1: *When Love Is a Lie*
*(Narcissistic Partners & the Pathological Relationship Agenda)*

#### #2: *Stop Spinning, Start Breathing*
*(Narcissistic Abuse Recovery: Managing the Memories That Keep Us Addicted)*

## Chapter X:
## Managing Down Our Expectations (MDOE)

For you, when the promised call never comes, nor does the next, it will feel as if you've been punched in the stomach. Any confidence you felt during the previous days or weeks of "love-bombing" is gone instantaneously as if you'd never felt a thing. In fact, you regret every second of that cocky confidence even though, in your heart, you know full-well he would have ditched you anyway. Or would he have? There's always that possibility that he was going *to stay* attentive and loving – and now you blew it by showing your mistrust. OMG, the Silent Treatment has begun. The anxiety comes over you like a wave. Is this going to last one week, two weeks, forever?? OMG, not the phone number too! What if he changes his number yet again, completely cutting you off, making you insane and unable to communicate your apologies? Frantically, you start calling his phone, only to hear it ring and ring and ring until it goes to voice mail. He doesn't call back but that's okay because you feel a quick sense of relief that at least the phone *is still on*. That's a *good sign*...okay, now you wait.

As the minutes tick by, the anxiety slowly builds again. You think about all the crazy, wonderful sex you just had and you panic. How can he make love to you like that and just walk out minutes later never to return? Another flash of relief as you get angry but it only lasts a minute before panic ensues. Where is he right now? Maybe something happened….yeah, that's it, something happened and he just hasn't had a chance to call. You bargain with your feelings – and with your logic. Deep down you know it's been two days and he should have called…after all, it only takes a second, right? You know that it has all begun again and that the pain will worsen with each passing day. You feel betrayed, raped, beat up, fooled, stupid. He did it again, that motherfucker. The thought of, well, maybe even a whole month of feeling overwhelming anxiety, wondering if he'll return, begging him to talk to you, leaving notes on his car, on his door, sending by mail. You didn't get the last word! He *always* gets the last word – without fail and every single fucking time! He set you up, he tricked you. And at the same time that you want him to just show up, you wish he would die.

What the narcissist does particularly well and with steadfast precision is *manage down our expectations (MDOE)* over time so that we expect less and less and he gets away with more and more. For him, the energy expended to get us back must, at some point, become next to nothing or we become *worth nothing*. MDOE is something that an N starts from almost day one and definitely from the first fight forward. He will work this slowly and methodically over many years, ensuring that the crumbs of attention needed to lure you back to the game are kept as low as they can go. Sure, in the beginning, he may have to fight just a wee bit harder to lure you back, but the rewards (later) are so huge in his narcissist world.

You see, when a "normal" partner *deliberately* expends more effort than needed in *any* part of the relationship, this is usually an indication of healthy predictability and well-intention. In such cases, the other partner, upon noticing the effort, naturally "ups" his or her expectations, thus keeping the momentum going. In a narcissist's world, the N *has no intention* of living up to anyone's expectations (but his own, of course) so *managing down* the expectations of those around him keeps him out of trouble. It's quite a brilliant strategy actually.

*Now, today is a good day. I did feel that twinge today - but only for a second - and then I started writing. I am a writer by trade and I spend many hours of my day writing for others. Today was the first time I actually wrote something that had nothing to do with anything except me. This minute, it feels very good. Tomorrow, I hope the same. Now when I am driving and I start to wonder where he is or what he is doing, I just think, "It doesn't matter where he is or what he is doing because, if he were here with you now, you know EXACTLY what he'd be doing - and it would just be another beginning to another horrible end...until the next time." This always moves me on to another thought. Realizing the fact that there will never be the closure we have been so desperately seeking has changed my level of anxiety. Not that I NEVER have the anxiety - it just exists at a cope-able level.*

*Six months ago, I couldn't see myself doing NC at all. I'd read about it, know it was the only way, yet never even attempt it. Then, within the past two months, he did one or two things that - believe it or not - I actually found unforgivable (even though they were no worse than any of his other abusive antics) to the point that I could ignore the phone calls and the pounding at the door. It happened without me really thinking about it. Like my time for NC had come. I'm not silly enough to think that I will*

141

*never see him again. He will surface. My friend said to me yesterday, "Make sure it's over for you because we all know that - as always - it is NOT over for him." So, every day is a work-in-progress.*

The things that the N won't do for you and with you are amazing. Normal responsibilities put him out, cramp his style, and become intolerable. He shirks all obligations to you, his family, and, eventually, to whomever he works for. Nothing is ever his fault – ever. He feels a *false sense of entitlement* every day, all day and there's no convincing him otherwise. He *hates to cooperate and compromise.* In fact, it kills him.

*Oh yes, mine chooses to live in a hotel (and not a nice one) and complain about the daily rent rather than get an apartment. In fact, he hasn't paid "rent" in over a year. He'd stay at his mom's until she'd demand money and then he'd move on to his dad. When his dad kicked him out, he'd come here and have a pocketful of cash while I struggled to pay the bills. When I finally lost it and demanded money, he'd pack his stuff up and stomp out - after being here months - and move on to whoever happened to be left out of his friends. He fully expected to live for free everywhere since, well, he was "saving" for an apartment. Once in awhile he'd buy something - toilet paper or food - but it was all about him and not helping. Disgusting, selfish behavior no matter how you look at it.*

*I couldn't believe the audacity of him moving out and immediately paying $40.00/night to a hotel rather than helping me with a couple of bills. Oh yes - like you said - then he'd stay at the hotel or at friends for* *free and still want to come hang out here! God, I hate him. It's these things that I remember that make me sick to my stomach. Every ugly thing - and every nice thing - they ever did was always part of a bigger plan to benefit their pathetic, self-absorbed lives. Calculation and manipulation - it's simply what they DO. Thanks, girlfriend! I'm so glad you wrote. I too hope that I keep writing - especially when I am feeling that weird little twinge that always leads to trouble. You have made me feel welcome. We deserve to forgive ourselves. It is the only way forward!*

I cannot tell you how many times I felt caught off guard with a kick to the curb. *And just when I thought there were no boundaries left for him to cross,* he'd find another or simply sideswipe an old one.

The first initial weeks of any given reconnect were always the same – lots of sex and me crying and accusing him of everything I knew (but couldn't prove) that he done while on vacation from me. The N, in turn, would adamantly offering illogical explanations for his behavior while at the same time working frantically behind the scenes to neatly tidy up the mess he just created by dumping someone to get back with *me.*

You see, whatever you just suffered during the last Discard is *exactly* what another girl/guy is going through *right now* while he weasels his way back into your bed and your life. Exactly. He has to completely cut himself off (only this time *from her*) – at least temporarily – from that other life that he always eventually returns to. The N is *never* alone during a separation although he will tell you that he is. It's a blatant, fucking lie and don't you believe it. Chances are that he even *lives* with someone else when he doesn't live with you. I saw the signs *so many times* when he'd come creeping back. The phone number changes again, he finds another apartment, moves on to a new job, stops talking to his family....blah blah blah. In the end, the N becomes nothing if not completely predictable.

Eventually, when the N felt comfortable and confident that his two, three, or more "relationship realities" wouldn't collide and ruin his fun, I'd feel comfortable and confident enough to settle back into my own private narcissist relationship hell for a few months or for as long as he could keep up the façade. The N kept me *so busy* worrying about the chaotic events of *each new day* that I would automatically place his most recent indiscretions on the back burner. This too, of course, was all part of the plan.

*To everyone - I am so grateful to have finally written. Susan said it so well - I have never seen so many amazing, intelligent voices in one place - EVER! It just goes to show how absolutely evil is the core of the N/P/S and how adept they are at their game to have sucked us in. What they do is so illogical, so amazingly deceitful, and so opposite of the truth - we are constantly shaking our head going, "No, it just can't be", trying to figure it out, trying to make sense of the nonsensical, struggling to fill in the blanks of even the smallest story, trying to find the goodness in there SOMEWHERE. Time just passes. We don't want to give up - not YET. We want to believe them - this ONE last time. We keep using "our history together" as an excuse to continue when, in actuality, there isn't any. We figure, "Well, he's here with me now...must be okay." To our credit, since we never really know EVERYTHING about what we feel is "off", we try not to make mountains out of molehills. Unfortunately, they know this and therefore know EXACTLY what they can get away with.*

Although Ns are incapable of feeling remorse, they will, invariably, have the uncanny ability to mimic appropriates emotion when they need to. As my relationship with the N moved forward and his mask began to slip, my N was not nearly as good at mimicking emotions as he had been in the early years. Or maybe I was just becoming better and quicker at catching it, who knows? Towards the end, when my N had to feign sadness of some sort, he learned to actually push out a tear when he needed to – but *just one tear*, mind you, and *only out of one eye*! No matter how hard he tried, he just couldn't push a tear out of *both* eyes at the same time – and it completely gave him away. I mean, it just looked *wrong*. As the years passed, even his disappearances and reappearances were conducted with less fanfare simply because my heart was too weary. [*NOTE: Many victims of narcissist abuse will tell you that, eventually, they actually come to welcome the Silent Treatments and Discards because it means getting a reprieve from the pain of being in the relationship (even if just for awhile). I, too, experienced this shift and, for me, it was a turning point in my favor – and he hated it.*]

It wasn't easy to start this book but once I got on a roll, I stayed up for almost three days straight. I've been a full-time writer for many, many years and never in my life did the words come so fast and so furiously. There was no stop and start, no lack of things to say, no disorganization like there would normally be in a book's first draft.

145

Nope, it was all smooth sailing – and it was, I admit, an exhausting but cathartic journey.

Look, I think we all *know* what we're supposed to be doing. *Of course,* we're supposed to be holding strong with No Contact. Since we can't legally murder these bastards, NC is the only way to rid ourselves of this evil. Eventually, one day - and hopefully before the best years of our lives pass by. I pray for each and every one of us. That being said, how do we get through the "now" time? During the time that these posts were written, I was always searching for a book that talked to me from a place of still being "there", with the guy, putting up with his shit, having sex with him, maybe asserting control here and there (and certainly paying for it), getting stronger but not strong enough to cut the ties, not being the best mom I could be and feeling the guilt…all of that…but I could never find a book that talked to me that way. So I decided to write one.

My thought is that you're probably still with the N as you read this – and that's okay. At least you're here reading, right? The fact that you've suspected *something* sinister shows that you've got one foot on the right path (even if the other *is* firmly planted in narcissist-hell). Or perhaps you've gone NC and fallen off the wagon (again). That's okay too. Breaking NC is not the end of the world, it's only the end of NC. The wagon will just sit there until you climb back on - as many of us have over and over.

Breaking NC is only catastrophic each time because, going back in, you already *know* that the Discard the next time around will always be worse than the one you just suffered through. The "knowing" is what truly sucks.

*Lying by omission - I hate that the most, I think. Even when I had completed my own investigations and discovered the truth, so much time had passed since "the omission", that I let it go, telling myself, "I'll just keep that discovery in the back of my mind until the perfect moment..." but that gratifying, perfect moment never comes because the N is always one step ahead with yet another unexpected Devalue & Discard (D & D). For me, the only way to get any peace at all (besides the closure that we imagine which will never happen) is to cast the burden, surrender all of it, give it up to a higher power. This has nothing to do with God, really, because everyone's higher power is different.*

*I started looking into Zen Philosophy years back and it really helped me feel okay about letting go, giving up expectation, and allowing detachment. Easier said than done? OMG, yes. But if we want to move forward, it is the only way. And to Susan... don't give up on trusting. These people are SO genuinely evil that they will NEVER EVER know happiness. And I'm glad! I know it seems like they go on with their merry lives but they don't. It's impossible. It really is. Find comfort in that if you can. For whatever reason - we came into contact with "bad seeds". "Bad seeds" cannot be fixed and they cannot be destroyed. They are what they are. However, they CAN be discarded - just like they do to us - and NC is the way to do it. As scary as it is and as sad as it makes me, I know now this is true.*

For many of you reading this, my words will address *the now,* the middle, the center of the knot that is your relationship with a narcissist. Although my words will validate you in that way, you must not misunderstand me - I am *not,* in any way, condoning or validating the existence of an abusive, life-threatening relationship *with anyone.* I'm going to trust that all who come to read my book and others will know what's up and what we're supposed to do. *We're all grown-ups and NC is the only way!* The truth is that I have no real message except maybe to say that *it sucks being in it until we can get out of it – and, eventually, we all do need to get out.*

I learned so much by studying the monster...his traits, my reactions, my kid's reactions, his reactions to my kid, me pulling myself out of slumps (and working myself into them), just how far his evil could take him and vice versa, the endless crossing of boundaries, what I *thought* he was doing and what I *knew* he was doing and how I figured it out, what I *never* figured out, the cell phone game, the internet game, his own dysfunctional family dynamic with a narcissistic and supposedly abusive mother, the sad loss of his father (not to death but to an illness) after which the narcissist was accountable to *no one* (let alone me!) and dropped what little of his evil mask was left completely, his curiosity about narcissism (when I called him on it) and his weird fascination with his own disorder, how he attempted to "use" his disorder as an excuse for cheating and lying, the back and forth, the D & D with which we are all so familiar, The Silent Treatment, how I studied him so hard that I could predict every single move and every single lie before it happened, the false sense of entitlement, how I've watched the

Narcissist slow with age and how living The Lie really does finally wear these assholes down at some level, how he will never ever change and we will never ever win and how our need to win (and to have closure) is what keeps us here clinging to nothing and wasting our best years, how we must forgive ourselves and how *the hell do we do that*, how do we get frigging *past it*, and how the end of this sad fairytale can only be written by me, by you, by us...not ever by them.

They have no intention of *ever ending this story* - and they have all the narcissistic time in the world to play it out a million different ways for their amusement....That, my sisters and brothers, is life as we know it in the belly of the beast.

#### ####

**I hope you enjoyed this excerpt from *When Love Is a Lie*. The full version is available in paperback and in Kindle from Amazon.com**

**Be sure to visit Zari's blog:**
**www.thenarcissisticpersonality.com**

# #2 STOP SPINNING, START BREATHING

## Exercise 1b:
### *Lies, Lies, Lies*

I emphasized it in **When Love Is a Lie** and I'll emphasize it again right now: narcissists lie even when the truth is a better story. Everything about the relationship itself and as a whole is false…a fabrication….a big fat lie. This habit of the narcissist to lie about everything - no matter what it is or how significant - is the core of our pain…..the nucleus around which our tears revolve day after day after day. My thought is that developing relationship amnesia is just one way our brain protects us from having to obsess about the past even more than we already do. But now….now that we're here trying to recover from the whole mess, we have to focus on all of it, including the lies. Not obsess, but focus. And that's why this section is about putting the relationship in its proper perspective. So, what better way to do that than to talk about all those lies?

How strange that, as soon as the relationship is over, we can't, for the life of us, remember why the narcissist is bad, bad, bad. All we can think about is the great sex or the last time he made us laugh or how long we've been "together" or how cute he is or whatever. Certainly, under normal circumstances, there wouldn't be a problem with thinking back on good times and cherishing certain parts of the relationship. But these are not normal circumstances. The fact is that none of what we remember as being good was ever real. Maybe those moments felt good to us right then but goodness is supposed to last longer than a moment. For the narcissist, nothing – not a single part of it - was real because he/she felt nothing. I know that's hard to wrap your head around but it's the truth.

This exercise is, again, about remembering the relationship as it truly was…the reality of it. While you're hurting, it's so easy to wrap the sadness of the situation in a delusional light but "delusional" is not what we want to be or how we want to feel right now. We want to be clear in our minds about what we just encountered…..the ·abuse…the manipulation…and, most importantly, the lack of reciprocated love. Unfortunately, we loved someone who was clearly not only unlovable lovable but unworthy as well and we need to accept that and have a clear picture of it. No more relationship amnesia or selective memory. No more sugarcoating the abuse and offering mental forgiveness before it's due. Now, I know there will be a certain number of readers – just as there were with my first book - who will insist that I don't hold myself accountable for anything. I, of course, know that that is a crock of shit and this isn't about accountability anyway – at least for this moment. It's about betrayal and pain and a broken heart. It's about the butterflies in your gut that never go away and the anxiety, the wondering, and the anger.

In order to heal, we simply must set aside the tears for right now and put the relationship in its proper perspective. Are you ready to begin?

1. *Once, when he disappeared for two weeks...simply vanished...he finally hovered with a text (as usual) saying he had flown back east to visit his sick father for two weeks and had just gotten back. LIE! I insisted that I saw his car around town but he insisted otherwise. LIE! Tickets, please. Nope, he said he'd thrown them out. LIE!*

2. *When he first came back around after being gone for three months and wanted to see me, he was going to come over but called to say his mother had had a stroke and was in the hospital and he couldn't make it. He even faked crying the entire call except he forgot to fake it right at the end, letting his voice completely go back to normal right as he hung up and I caught it. A call to every hospital in town confirmed what I knew. LIE!*

3. *When he'd moved of his apartment and swore up and down he was homeless and living in his truck. However, when he'd call, I could tell he was in someone's house and even heard voices in the background that he denied were there. It would take him a long to call me back if I left a message. Many other things led me to believe otherwise. LIE!*

**Now it's your turn. Looking back, write a few paragraphs, each describing a fictitious story, fabricated excuse, a lie by omission, or just an out and out lie told to you**

by the Narcissist at any point in your relationship. The lie's level of significance isn't important because a lie is still a lie. Feel free to write out as many as you can remember. Fill up a whole damn notebook if you like. This is a time to purge no matter how painful the memory.

---

---

---

---

---

This – the endless lying – is at the heart of the emotional suffering that we endured and that is a fact. To expect us to "just get over it" is not only ludicrous, it's completely unrealistic. Being lied to over and over and over by someone we love is the ultimate betrayal and breeds general mistrust all around. The affects of the narcissist's lies spill into other areas of our lives and disrupt the normal flow of everyday life. It affects our children and our families. Without a doubt, I feel that this is the most damaging part of the narcissist's pathological relationship agenda and the more we purge...the more we accept and release the words of the betrayal, the lighter our hearts will be.

# Exercise 1c:
## *Navigating Cognitive Dissonance*

By most definitions, cognitive dissonance is the psychological discomfort or torment a person feels when he or she holds conflicting beliefs about something simultaneously. On other words, we are torn between believing what we want to believe and accepting what we know to be the truth about someone or something. It happens to everyone numerous times in a lifetime and oftentimes will result in our making an important decision that ultimately works in our best interest or for the best interest of our family.

Cognitive dissonance is not always a bad thing because it helps us weigh both sides of a situation and make (hopefully) the best choice based on the truth and on the facts. Cognitive dissonance is not always a bad thing, that is, until it becomes the catalyst for our inability to leave a narcissistic partner or to remain in a state of "no contact" or to not give in to the hovering or to recover from the whole ordeal when it is finally is really truly over. It becomes a problem when it keeps us shackled to a codependency to hope that will never get us anywhere as long as we choose to remain chained.

The hardest part about letting go of the narcissist is our reluctance to accept what we already know to be true – that nothing about anything we experienced in our own mind was real.....that he didn't love us (never did and never will)....that every precious moment, every kiss and caress...all those times when we really thought it was coming around and oh-how-glad-we-were-that-we-stuck-it-out....that all those times were LIES. It was all fake, a fabrication created by the **narcissist** to benefit the narcissist. All those things that we miss – the sayings, the gestures, the witty comments – were falsities....clever workings of a con artist who knew how to present his stuff in a way that tugged at our heartstrings. So, not only do we suffer relationship amnesia when it's over, we suffer selective relationship amnesia, remembering only the best of the best in high definition and with all the sounds and smells in tact as well. No doubt, cognitive dissonance is a bad trick the brain plays on those already suffering the grief of love lost. And, yes, it is very sad.

The fact, unfortunately, is that the narcissist hates you, me, and anyone who truly has a heart. He hates us because we are capable of loving. He has hated us from the day we became his target. Oh, but that wasn't true the *whole* time, was it? Yup, it was. Just think about it. While you may not want to believe it, how many times did he climb out of your bed early after great sex, giving some illogical excuse for the departure and disappear for two unexplainable days ...just vanishing into thin air? You get my point. In fact, the N probably did that or something similar to you many times over the years. And what about the sex? Ohhh yes, *the sex*. For me, *the sex* was my *everything*. How could he not love me if the sex was so great? That just wasn't possible! So, okay, he does a million bad things that scream hatred towards me but I'm going to cling to the sex and pretend that *that's* how he *really* feels. Sure, that makes sense. Or does it? And so it goes….our cognitive dissonance sends us to hell and back once again. Struggling to accept that your entire relationship was a fake even though you know in your heart of hearts that it was….wanting to believe that the narcissist must have loved you at some point in the relationship even though you know that no one who loved you would have *ever* done the things that he did to you (and behind your back).

The one belief that saved me from dying from a broken heart throughout my 13-years with a narcissist motherfucker is my belief that all things have to be, for the most part, logical in order to be true. In other words, something has to make sense before I believe it. Towards the end of my relationship, when I couldn't take it anymore…the constant lying and the constant insult to my intelligence, I started tossing out the same response to his word salad: "I'm sorry, but that's not logical, Wayne. It couldn't have happened that way. You're lying" and it absolutely infuriated him. And since he had no intention of ever telling me the truth, he simply started mocking me about it – "Logical, logical, logical…I'm sick of your "logical" bullshit!" and he'd mock me all the way out the door and then, of course, he'd vanish.

You can't argue with logic. You just can't. I used logic to navigate my way through – and up and out of – the muddy waters of cognitive dissonance. And you can too, my friends. In order to wake from a narcissistic nightmare, you must start observing the processes of your recovery logically. Things that make sense are good for you and the narcissist, as we know, is completely nonsensical. We can't keep postponing our recovery based on conflicting beliefs about the narcissist – especially when we know the truth. Unlike a narcissist, we know right from wrong.

To escape the grief and emotional torment of cognitive dissonance, you have to choose between the two beliefs and using logic is one way to ensure that you make the right choice.....for yourself, for your children, for your future, and for your sanity.

This exercise is about recognizing your level of cognitive dissonance and understanding that there really is a name for all those conflicted feelings.....and I'll go first:

*Even though I know now it wasn't real, I still miss the way he'd hold my face in his hands when he kissed me.*

*Even though I know now he didn't mean it, I still liked it when he told me that he thought I was a really smart person.*

*Even though I know now it would have never happened, I still wish we could have grown old together like he always said he was sure would happen.*

*Even though I know now it was just a ploy, I still laugh when I think about how he would "affectionately" mimic some of my more dramatic mannerisms.*

*Even though I know he could care less about me, I can't help but hold on to the belief that surely he must think of me and my son many times in a day.*

*Even though he'd done it to me a thousand times and I have absolutely no reason to believe that the next time would be any different, I can't help but think that maybe he really has changed and finally he can stop with this bad behavior, realize what a good catch I am, and love me like I deserve to be loved.*

In the section below, I've started a few sentences that you can finish in any way that you want. You'll notice that I start each sentence under the premise that you *already know* that the things that you miss about the N are a falsehood. I've also provided some blank areas as well where you can develop similar sentences on your own based on the pieces of your own experience Again, writing things down – even though it can be bittersweet – is a great way to release the mental image of the lie itself and, so, with this exercise, we'll deliberately allow ourselves a few more nostalgic moments. To navigate the waters of cognitive dissonance, we have to resolve to the fact that whatever we thought was real in the relationship never was. When love is a lie, we simply have no choice but to make the right choice lest we sentence ourselves to waste what's left of our life as well. And be proud of yourself in the process because it's a monumental step in starting over.

Even though I know now it wasn't real, I still miss:

Even though I know now his feelings weren't genuine, I still liked it when:

_____

_____

_____

Now feel free to make up your own sentences representing the cognitive dissonance you feel about your relationships – the untruths that you can't let go of....the "wishes" for things that you know in your heart wouldn't have or will not ever happen. It is our understanding of the difference that gives us the strength to let go of a relationship that, for all intents and purposes, existed in our imagination. When we finally "get" this, then and only then can we being to break our codependency to hope and, consequently, our attachment to the narcissist.

_____

_____

_____

To begin recovery, we have to decompress and deprogram ourselves from the brainwashing of narcissism. We have to learn to make the right choices and to come to terms with our conflicting beliefs about the person that is hurting us. Once we do that, things start to calm down. Being confused about our feelings…knowing one thing to be true yet *feeling* something totally different is exhausting and will wear your moral, self-esteem, and overall self worth into the ground before you even know what's happening.

Keep an eye on your cognitive dissonance because, if the problem is a narcissist, I am certain you've been struggling with it. Keep your beliefs about this person in check at all times and you will start to see the forest for the trees. Things will go from dark to light and the narcissistic fog he has placed over your life will slowly start to lift. Being mindful of *you* at all times is the only real way of working through the pain.

#####

**I hope you enjoyed this excerpt from *Stop Spinning, Start Breathing*. The full version is available in paperback and in Kindle from Amazon.com.**

**Be sure to visit Zari's blog:**
**www.thenarcissisticpersonality.com**

Made in the USA
Lexington, KY
28 May 2019